LESLIE
F*CKING
JONES

LESLIE F*CKING JONES

A MEMOIR

LESLIE JONES

FOREWORD BY CHRIS ROCK

GRAND
CENTRAL

NEW YORK   BOSTON

To all the people who loved me . . .

To all the people who hated or hurt me . . .

To all the people who had my back and looked out . . .

You know who you are.

Thank you.

I dedicate this book to you. Without you, I wouldn't be Leslie Fucking Jones.

I love you Willie, Diane, and Keith.

Foreword

When Leslie Jones walks into a room, she's always out of breath and mad about something. Whenever you see her, you always feel like you just missed a fistfight. And she won.

But, as successful as she is, I have to say, I don't like the way Hollywood has treated her. She's too funny not to be *every*where, in *every* movie, on *every* TV show, with ten Netflix specials. She should already have been a Marvel villain, or an animatronic version of herself in a Guardians of the Galaxy movie. She should already have had a franchise action series, with towering billboards, a gun barrel by her cheek, and her side-eye cocked and loaded. Even in drama she would have been a great Harriet Tubman, and she kinda looks like Nina Simone.

I've known the lady for twenty years, and let me let you in on a secret: Back then, nobody wanted her. She was just going around the circuit, cracking the earth up, but Hollywood was not interested. Yes, Hollywood is that dumb.

Then one day, Lorne Michaels called me looking for a funny Black woman. And here's a little insight into the workings of Hollywood. *SNL*, the American capital of comedy, has no idea where to find funny Black people. Not their fault. Just how it is. *SNL* knows where to find funny *white* people because they have things called *institutions*. You can find funny white people at Harvard, The Groundlings, The Second City . . .

Funny Black people are usually working at your local DMV.

So, when Lorne called, I said, "You gotta get Leslie Jones! There is nobody like her. She's hilarious."

And then, admittedly, I used her height to cover my ass in case she tanked. I said, "Lorne, I guarantee that she will stand out among the cast. She will be head and shoulders above everybody else."

To be honest, I said, "Lorne, hire her or make her your nanny, what do you care? You're Lorne Michaels."

Lorne hired her off my word alone, and now she's a household name. And you know what that means? She owes me some money.

So I'm gonna count every book she sells, and if this hilariously funny memoir becomes a bestseller, I want a check.

—Chris Rock

SNL

The gig was in Indianapolis; I was second billing, but I knew how it would go. As soon as the headliner—a guy I knew—saw my name, he'd make up some excuse to go ahead of me. I was hard to follow. I'd been doing comedy since 1987; now, it was 2013, and I was tired of this shit. Flying in, doing a show, getting $1,000, maybe $1,500, being bumped to headliner without getting paid more . . . And all because these pieces of shit make up some crap about having to drive home in the snow.

Sure enough, about an hour before the show, there was a knock on my door. I opened it, and there was one of the promoters.

"So, the weather is really bad, and the headliner has to drive back. You have to go last."

I said nothing.

"The thing is," he said, "he has to drive . . ."

"Give me a thousand more," I said.

"But you're all getting paid the same, and you're all doing the same time—"

"No, we're not," I said. "The spot you want me to take is headliner. Not the same. So, if you got a thousand dollars more, then I'll headline, but if not, then y'all got a problem."

Back then, I didn't work the road during the week, which meant from Thursday to Monday I was hitting the clubs all over the country. I'd usually do at least four or five shows— some weekends it was seven, and most of the time the money wasn't good. With a schedule like that, you just hope you can sell merchandise afterwards to make it worth it. People don't know that's our life; and that's why I was going to fight for my money that night and every night.

"A thousand more? I'm not going to do that," the promoter said.

I just looked at him blankly and started packing up my shit. These promoters are all janky, slick-ass muthafuckas, often drug dealers or the "big guy" in town, always with the greased-back hair or Jheri curl; nice suit sometimes, or maybe a sweat suit. Chain. Bottle of liquor in his hand. Their job is to give as little money to the comedians as possible. *Go fuck yourself.*

"Well, then I guess I'm going back to the hotel room, cuzz. I don't play this shit, homey," I said.

"You're just going to walk out?" he squealed.

"Listen," I said, walking up to him to make sure he realized I was at least a foot taller than he was. "You obviously don't know me. You shouldn't be making this decision yourself. You should go back and talk to the other promoter. The one that hired me and who does, indeed, know me."

And I turned back to keep packing up my stuff, and off he went.

In my head, I slowly counted to five. I was really starting to understand my power at this point of my career. Then I heard footsteps running along the hallway. The first promoter, and the guy who knew me, arrived at my door.

"Here's your money!" the promoter who knows me said. "I'm sorry for the confusion . . . It won't happen again."

When he'd finished making excuses, I put my hand on top of the money and said, "Let me explain something to you. That was some bullshit that dude fed you. And I'm going to tell you right now, he'll be sitting in the audience, watching my show, after he has told you he needs to drive home."

The business was filled with so many of these chauvinistic pieces of shit. I knew what they said about me: "If she thinks she's so funny, see if she can follow me . . . The crowd think that joke's funny because *she* did it, but watch *me* do it." Everybody thought I was a fluke. But I knew I wasn't just lucky; I'd been in the same gutters as these muthafuckas. I'd ripped the same rooms they'd ripped. I knew I was the real deal.

I did the headlining gig for the extra thousand. By the time I went up, the crowd was drunk and unruly, and sure enough, right there in the crowd was the headliner who I'd switched with. The guy looked like an asshole. His face seemed to say, "Go on then, bitch, try and rip these drunk muthafuckas," until I started to rip, and then his attitude changed. He looked like a kid when something bad has happened and he's been caught. Imagine two dogs—the first dog is impatient and eats the tiny treat, but the second dog waits and gets the chicken wing.

I was the second dog.

I killed—but then, I always killed. That was never the problem. The fans are always what give me life.

Back at the hotel after the show, I called my manager.

"I can't keep doing this shit," I said.

"I hear ya," he said. Then he told me something he really didn't need to tell me right then. "And I don't mean to make you sad or whatever, but I don't think they going to pick you for the *SNL* thing either, dude."

"I get it," I said. "I get it."

I felt defeated. Everything felt played out. What's next? What the fuck is next?

———————

Chris Rock had gotten me the *SNL* audition.

Every time I would see Chris at a club, I would wait by the door until he was done, and then as he left, I'd chase him all the way out to his car.

"I don't know why the fuck you not hooking me up," I'd say. "Why you not telling people I'm funny? I'm not going to make it unless somebody like you tells them I'm funny."

And Chris would look at me, smile, and he'd say, "You're not ready."

And I'd say to myself, *How the fuck do you know if I'm ready or not?* How much more ready could I be? I'd been doing this shit for twenty years. How much more ready can a bitch be? Has he not heard how I've been ripping these rooms? Shit.

As his car would roar away, I would say to myself, "Fuck you! You don't know what the fuck ready is."

But I *wasn't* ready, though—I had not gone to the next level with my jokes yet.

I started chasing Chris around 2005. But it wasn't until after my brother died in November 2009 that I finally started doing the stuff I wrote years earlier but never performed. You have to go through shit to really connect to your material, or have a point of view. I was always writing jokes I thought I would do eventually when I was funny enough to perform them. But mostly I thought I was writing for someone else. I would tell myself, *These smart jokes are too smart for you.* How fucking stupid—I didn't understand I was writing material for myself, but saying I couldn't perform it.

I'd written my very first real joke in 1997. I didn't use it in my set until 2010. When I wrote it, I thought, *Whoopi's going to do that joke, because she's going to turn that into something else. Or maybe it's for Marsha Warfield—Marsha Warfield is going to kill that joke . . .*

Like I said, fucking stupid.

I came up with the idea for that joke after I did something I swore I'd never do again. I had a rule: nothing goes before God, comedy, or family, in that order. But I broke my rule by turning down a gig because I was waiting for a guy. I had already hooked up with him once, and I was planning on hooking up with him again. I was supposed to do a gig at Luna Park, which for a while was one of the popular music venues in Los Angeles. The promoter of the comedy night, Greg "Gee Mack" Dalton, had even promised to come and pick me up and everything, but I was determined to wait on the guy I wanted to hook up with. But that guy never showed up, and I missed the gig. Waiting for him was one of the worst decisions I ever made. And me missing that gig fucked up an opportunity for me to host Luna Park—they offered it to another comedian. I vowed that dick would never fuck up my shit again.

Later that same week, I went on another disastrous date with someone else, and afterwards I was just sitting in the middle of the floor of my apartment, eating cold Chinese food out of a carton. I was just mad. And the joke came to me: If we were back in the slave days, I would be considered a top slave, the number one slave draft pick. I'm six foot tall; I'm healthy; I have all my own teeth, and they're nice and white; I'm strong; and who knows, I'm probably really fertile, like the Nile.

By this point, I'm rolling laughing. But there's more:

The plantation owners would be giving me only the best Black men, because they wanted only the best Black offspring. I would never be single. They would consider me a Mandingo, and they would be bringing me Mandingos.

I would be getting all the fine-ass slaves—the *Denzels*. And then every nine months I would shoot out a champion.

Then I mimed shooting a baby out of me.

"Shaq. Kobe. Kimbo Slice. Prince . . . Nah, you're not done yet," and I'd stuff Prince right back in.

I didn't perform that joke for ten years. Then my brother died in November 2009, a month before his birthday. Until death touches you directly, it doesn't fully impact you. I had been prepared for my parents' deaths, but my brother's death came out of nowhere. Before that, as a performer I was like a wild bucking horse. I didn't have a foundation to my jokes; I was silly onstage, clown-like. I was doing stuff I thought *I* would laugh at—there's nothing wrong with that, but my set was all over the place. It was a set just to make money. But in the back of my mind, I knew I had these main jokes that I'd worked on, even though I hadn't been ready to perform them.

But after my brother died, it was like a sheet got pulled back. Nothing was as colorful as before. I had woken up; shit is real. You better live because muthafuckas be dyin'. I wanted to do jokes I had never done before. I needed to find joy again. I need to feel like I'm eating steak, not rabbit food. So I started doing hard shit. Figuring it out.

Whenever I would do the slave joke at the Parlor on Melrose, it would kill. The Parlor was one of my favorite places to perform because Jay Davis, who ran the room, had a great audience. It was a white, industry audience, but they were hipsters, liberal and with it. *They going to let me be this real in a white club?* Hell yeah—and every time I did that joke, there was one white guy with eighties rock-band hair who was in the industry, and he would always come up to me.

"That is just brilliant," he'd say. "You could see the pain, but you could also see the comedy. It's so good."

Finally, one night in late 2013, I did the joke at the Comedy Store, late spot. When I said "Kimbo Slice," the audience lost it.

It was midnight. In the back of the room, my close friend Owen Smith was watching me kill with the slave joke and noticed that Chris Rock was standing at the door. Owen said that when I finished, he saw Chris take out his phone and type something.

Owen went over to him and said, "Chris, what you putting in your phone?"

"She just went on my funny people list," Chris said.

(Later, Owen told me he said, "Chris! Don't leave! Watch me do my shit and put me on your funny list too!")

From there, Chris had dinner with Lorne Michaels and mentioned me to him. Chris then called me to tell me somebody from *Saturday Night Live* would be contacting me.

"Why the fuck would you do that?" I said. "I'm not a sketch comedian. I'm a stand-up. I'm not going to be able to do that shit—"

"Shut the fuck up," Chris interrupted. "Go out there and do stand-up. Be funny. I don't want to hear this shit. Bye." And then he hung up.

So, I guess I had to fly to New York.

To a lot of people back then, I was still just the "lucky Black girl," "the fluke." But let me tell you something—I was forty-seven. I'd lived. I wasn't some kid. And I was already a fucking dope-ass comic. No one could fuck with me; the likes of the shady headliners were always begging not to follow me because they knew they couldn't. I was ready—everybody knew that Leslie was not to be fucked with onstage.

Everyone says *SNL* is like going to college to learn how to do comedy with other people at the top of their game. So, when the call came to audition for *SNL*, I was like, *If this is college, I'm already a comedy graduate.* I was going to make them hire me. Like, they'd have no choice.

I was going to make myself undeniable.

Chapter One

QUANTUM LEAP

have this recurring idea. I want to quantum leap back to my younger self and tell that person all the stuff she needs to hear. I was standing in my closet recently, looking at my clothes, and realized that the only person who could truly appreciate all this shit, and what it took to get here, is me. (There's a reason I called my last Netflix special *Time Machine*.) I used to go to the mall whenever I got a bit of money, but back then I'd just buy everything in black—I'd have a closet filled with black clothes only, and jeans and T-shirts. These days? Beautiful gowns, jackets, lingerie, swimsuits—it's like a department store, but a really exclusive, high-end one. There are clothes in there I haven't even worn yet! Sometimes I'll look at that closet and say, "Who do you think you are, Diana Ross?"

When I think about how far I've come, I want to go back through my life and give my former self the love and respect

1

she so often missed out on. I want to look after my younger me, tell her she'll be alright—better than alright.

She'll be *Leslie Fucking Jones.*

(But I'm also glad that I didn't ever get those positive notes from myself, because if I had, I might have been cocky, and without them, I still became Leslie Fucking Jones anyway.)

When I was in the sixth grade in Fort Bragg, I was around white kids a lot. I didn't think of myself as a Black kid; I was just a kid. The white kids didn't care, either; we were all just military kids. But their parents were the racist ones; some would refer to me as "Smut" or "Darky," and my friend's mother gave me the nickname "Blacky." I had no idea it was offensive.

One day, my mom found out that I'd been called Blacky, and she started crying. She knew I was innocent, didn't know what the fuck that meant.

My mother sat me down and explained how offensive this was; she felt bad about it, but she had to tell me what racism is, when I had been oblivious to it before that. All the kids were fucked up after that; I didn't want to play with my friend anymore. I now looked at people differently. Racism is *taught* to kids—they're not born that way.

I started thinking that maybe I was ugly because I was dark skinned, darker than other Black kids. And because my mom knew I was having a hard time with these feelings, she stepped in to save me—she got an African woman she knew to come to school to talk to me (my mom and dad both worked, and I barely remember not being at school—I was always there). Actually, she might have been just wearing African clothes . . . Either way, that's when I started believing in angels.

We met in the counselor's office. The African woman's skin was smooth, like chocolate. It was as if you could take your hand and dip it into her skin. She was elegant and smelled so good; her teeth were perfect. She was stunning.

"Am I going to look like you?" I said to my mom's friend.

Very calmly and kindly, the African woman looked me in the eyes and said, "You're actually going to be more beautiful than me."

I remember thinking, *No way.*

I can't tell you what a huge effect that had on me. Actually, I can: It changed my life. After that, I went around saying, "I'm a Black muthafucka, I'm blacker than you, I'm proud."

Forty years later, I'm Leslie Fucking Jones, but that lesson from that woman stays with me. Every time I go somewhere, there's always some pretty little Black girl who wants to connect. Recently, I went to a Keith Sweat concert, and sure enough, a Black girl and her mom came over to me. I could immediately see what the girl was feeling; I could immediately tell what she was going through.

"You're my favorite star," the girl said, "and you're so beautiful."

I've always been an empath. (When I'm onstage, I use it for crowd work—I'm careful to not go after someone unless

I'm pretty sure they can take it.) I saw myself in that little girl that night. I can tell when someone is wounded; I saw the pain; I imagined other kids making fun of her; I could tell she was embracing who she was a Black girl, but others weren't embracing it yet. She had clearly taken time to do her hair, and she was so proud of it, but I could imagine people making fun of her for it.

I could see that this girl was looking closely at me and my hair. It reminded me of the first time I saw Whoopi—back then I remember thinking, *That's me, grown up.* It had been the same with the African woman I'd spoken to all those years ago in grade school, too: *It's OK to look like me.*

I knew that girl needed to be told that she was going to be fine and on the right path. She was going to be greater sooner than I ever was.

I grabbed that little girl's face.

"*You* are beautiful," I said. I kissed her face, and I hugged her. And then I pulled her to one side, and I said, "I know it's hard right now. If you get through it, I swear to God, you're going to triumph better than anything. You're going to be so strong. You just gotta get through it. Hold on. It does not last. It's going to get better."

There's a lot of little girls who feel like that—shit, many grown-ass women feel like that. I've come to understand that that's what I'm here for, now—that's one of the reasons I'm on this planet: I was built to be strong, and I want to share it, pay it forward. And real talk: I was never a victim, even though really bad shit happened to me. I know it's my job to help other Black girls and women get strong like me.

Beneath all the stories you're about to read is this message: We have to take care of ourselves and realize the wonderfulness in all of us. Because once we start doing that, once we start with respecting ourselves—really getting into the business of liking ourselves—we'll realize that each of us is a unique person with God-given gifts that we have to use to the benefit of everyone around us. You are with yourself every day, all day, all night—might as well like yourself.

I've had to carve out a career as a woman—a *Black* woman—in a business where so many of the gatekeepers are white males. I've been told I'm not funny because I'm a woman; I've had people hire me and then want me to be someone I'm not; I've been subject to racism and sexism. But always, I believed in myself.

The first time I touched a mic onstage, I knew I was home. Eventually I built a successful career in comedy, and I did it by not compromising; by learning to love myself; by proving over and over that I'm tougher, smarter, and fucking funny. And I did it by realizing that the best comedy is built on a foundation of hard truths, of real talk, and real work. (Recently, when I was a guest on his talk show, Seth Meyers said, "Leslie, honesty is your main export.")

Hey you guys—some of the stories about my childhood are vague because a bitch is fifty-five and I've smoked a lot of weed. A lot of it is hazy, but I will give you the best recollection of it that I can. Every day I have to fight so that no one takes me for granted, and no one takes advantage. These are the stories that explain why. (Cue the *Law & Order* theme.)

———————

One of the people who taught me to make sure no one took me for granted was my father, Willie Jones Jr. He was an electronics engineer in the army—a genius at it, too. But I didn't see him much in my early years; I know now that he was off serving his country abroad. Back then, though, I had no idea he was risking his life because to me, Daddy was just Daddy. Recently, me and my uncle William Earl were talking about my dad, and I was amazed at some of the stuff he told me.

"He did Korea," William Earl said. "I did Korea with him, and Vietnam, too."

"You went back?" I said, hardly able to believe it.

"Yeah, man," he said, "everybody went back."

"But I thought Black men would be treated badly."

"Sometimes we were!" he said, "but in the army we were also brothers. We were always treated badly on bases in the States, but once we got overseas, things improved. Bullets coming at you change your attitude about color."

Everybody knew Willie Jones Jr—he hated to be called Willie Jones, because that was his dad's name, and he hated his dad. Willie Jones Jr was our light, our foundation. He was something. He didn't throw parties—he *was* the party. When he wasn't working, our house was the place to be on Fridays to listen to all his albums and have a fish fry. My mom, Sundra Diane, could fry the fuck out of a fish.

There was one night we started at a different house and picked up a family, then headed to the next house, picked up some more, before we finally arrived at my uncle's house, where the party was. Along the way, we were blasting the oldies, and at every stoplight we'd all jump out of the car and start dancing. Before the light changed, we all had to dive back in the car so we could keep going. We were a fun family.

For a while we lived in North Carolina because my dad was stationed at Fort Bragg, and sometimes we'd take a road trip to see family in Memphis. But we always traveled at night. Dad liked to drive through the darkness, and I would stay awake with him. (That's probably why I'm a night owl now.) Once in a while he'd catch eyes with me in his rearview mirror.

"You up?" he'd say.

"Yeah."

"You ready?"

"Yeah."

We both knew what this meant. He'd put on George Benson's "This Masquerade," which seemed like it was twenty minutes long. I was about five or six, maybe a bit older. And we would just sit back and listen and look out the window as America went by. I thought that was the most beautiful song. After the George Benson he would play Donny Hathaway and Al Green—man, just the music going through you . . .

We would always stay in the places that were fun, too. At the time, Ramada Inns had these theme hotels. Once, we were riding through a town, and we saw a castle.

My mind started racing. *If we stayed there, would I get a crown? Would there be swords?* I had to find out.

"Dad, please, please can we stay there?" I shouted.

"Only if it's a Ramada Inn," he said.

He only liked Ramada Inns because back then they were the best of the best, and my dad liked to give us the best of the best. (If we ate steak out, we ate the best steak.) So, we—me, my brother, my mom, my dad, and my grandmother—got a room at that Ramada Inn, and I drove everyone crazy running up and down the halls because it was a fucking castle.

———————

My mom and dad had been sweethearts in high school, in Memphis, Tennessee. My mom's mom abandoned her and her brother, Butch—literally left them on a street corner somewhere. I'm hazy on family details given that my mother was abandoned, and she never talked about it, but I'm pretty sure that Aunt Winnie was my grandmother's sister, and it was Aunt Winnie who raised my mom.

When I was a very little kid, before my brother was born, for a short time Aunt Winnie helped raise me, too. She lived on a farm in Jericho, Arkansas, about twenty minutes northwest of Memphis. I always sat in Winnie's lap to eat at the time. She'd make beautiful art out of egg cartons and those plastic rings from soda cans, too, and she kept snuff everywhere.

Jericho's just a street, less than half a mile square—not even two hundred people lived there, and almost all of us were Black. Aunt Winnie's farm was right across the street from the cotton fields and the railroad track that follows Route 77 through town. We used to walk those tracks.

One day I got my white socks dirty playing by the railroad, and I thought Winnie was going to spank me. They were really nice white socks, and she was always telling me to not get them wet.

By the time I got back to the farm, I was crying so hard.

"What's wrong, what's wrong?" Winnie asked, terrified that something terrible had occurred.

"I got my socks wet," I said in a tiny voice.

"Oh, girl," she said, "I can wash your socks! I thought something bad happened."

I think about that little girl now—the worst thing that could happen to her, ever, was that her socks got wet.

———————

My father liked to drink—a lot. If I'd known back then that my dad had gone to Korea, maybe I would've understood better why he drank so much.

In those early years, Dad was cool as fuck—not angry, just drunk and happy. His drinking didn't make him scary, though he was scary nonetheless because he was huge. He had a trumpet voice and he was 6'5". But I was glad he was that way. He was a sergeant and people respected him, and he was that muthafucka—you didn't want to really fuck up and get a whooping from him. But if something happened and Daddy had to whoop you, then you knew you had really fucked up. One day, I was terrorizing him—because that's what kids do—and he'd had enough. I had just done something really stupid and I was running away, and to slow me down he threw a shoe at me and got me right in the back of the head. He could really throw a shoe.

"Daddy!?" I shouted when the shoe hit me.

"That's what your ass gets for running," he said. Both of us fell out laughing at that. I always loved it when I made him laugh—it was usually when I did something I shouldn't be doing, like the time I fell all the way down the stairs—he thought *that* was hilarious.

Later, my aunt told me that he'd gotten way better after having us—he used to discipline his siblings all the time since he was the oldest.

My dad's dad beat the shit out of my dad and my grandmother. And then later, when my grandmother married her second husband, Ed, he literally tortured my dad, making it clear that he wasn't his kid. He would actually make my dad pick bones out of the tiny little fish they'd catch, and my dad would be crying because it was shitty, painful, humiliating, frustrating work, and then that man would give the fish to a white man anyway.

My dad had it hard growing up, because he was a Black man in white America. But he eventually got to a point where he was tall and athletic and strong. Trust and believe that they did not push Willie Jones Jr around anymore. Then, when he was nineteen and my mom was eighteen, I came along, so he joined the army to take care of his family. But despite being in the military, he still did his thing—he just was Willie Jones Jr.

My family faced racism all the time. My dad's mother, Big Mama as we lovingly call her in the family, got arrested for fighting back when three white boys tried to rape her—she was as tall as I am now and beat their asses. My great-grandfather had to go down to the jail with a gun to get her out, so my dad was born into that shit—all of them were.

My father hated white people, and I couldn't fault him for that after understanding where he came from—he thought white people were the devil and hoogees (not a word a white person has probably ever heard, nor anyone outside of the South, I bet). "I don't work with hoogees," he'd say. But white people . . . they, like everyone else, loved Willie Jones Jr.

My dad was very much against "the Man," for sure, but he was also clear about what life had in store for me. He knew I'd have to fight for everything I got.

"Don't let anyone tell you that you're Black and you're a woman and you can't do it," he'd say. "You can do whatever the fuck you want. As long as you work hard. But you have to work hard. You can't get the shit easy. As long as you are better than everybody else, you'll get what you deserve."

He was the one who said I had to be undeniable.

"You are Black; you are a woman." He said it every day. "But if you work harder and you're better than everybody else, you are undeniable. They can't deny you. They going to tell you that you are a woman, they're going to tell you that you're Black. Don't fucking listen."

I couldn't help but see the things he had to face, that we all had to face, and I would get so angry. (Often, people in my family call me Willie Jones Jr to this day—I have his voice, and his temper. I'm proud of that.)

Back then, for someone like my father there was no such thing as *Oprah*, or talk therapy, or sharing your feelings. Willie Jones Jr was very proud, and honestly, even if there had been someone who could have helped him with his demons, he probably wouldn't have taken the help anyway. So many of us try to do our own emotional oil change, but we're not mechanics. He had no help—he went to war, and he saw people die—and he drank. He drank and drank and drank.

A lot of stuff needs to be fixed between generations. Every generation thinks they have a new set of issues to deal with, when actually it's just a different scene, different clothes, different mechanisms, but the same damage getting passed down. And when no one talks about it—when people "forget"—nothing gets fixed. I just wish everybody would have a conversation about it. Every race goes through something—Black, white, Spanish, Asian . . . No one is free of fucked-upedness. We've all got baggage. But if we could just have some compassion for each other's baggage, everything could be solved so much differently. The older I get, the more compassion I have for Willie Jones Jr.

———————

Sundra Diane Brantley was the one who would keep us in check, the one who would fuck us up in a minute. My mom did not play that shit, which is funny, because she was a full Leo—very sweet. She was one of the most nurturing people I've ever known. Leos are so nurturing anyway, but my mom was just nurturing to a fault, even when it meant she could come off as a doormat. Sometimes she'd just do and do and do, help and help and help. She was always giving of herself to people. Muthafuckas would sometimes take advantage of her. But she wasn't no punk. Leos put up with a lot until they snap. She could be very vocal. You'd have hurt her feelings seven times before she would no longer fuck with you, but if you apologized, she'd fuck with you again.

But that didn't mean my mom was weak—she did not fucking play. She loved us—seriously, she loved her children—but if we fucked up, she would fuck us up. Those ass whoopings . . . maaaan, I deserved every one of them.

I had been a difficult birth for a start—my mother had struggled so hard, and it had been so stressful, that the doctor even forgot to write down the exact time of my arrival. (Shit, now I don't even know what cusp I'm on!) My mom had been so exhausted that when it came to telling the nurse my name for the paperwork, she'd just threw out the names, and the nurse put them in the order *she* wanted, so I was "Annette Leslie Jones." Growing up I was always "Leslie" to anyone who really knew me (except in high school, where people called me Annette). When my mother told me the story of my naming, I said I was going to get it changed officially.

"No way you doing that," she said. "Because that would mean I made a mistake, and I don't make mistakes."

Me and my kid brother, Rodney Keith (we called him Keith), were a lot, and when we were little, because my dad was always in the army, everything fell to her—she had to deal with all of our shit. I don't know how that woman didn't kill us—Lord have mercy, how did she not smother us with a pillow?

My mom was supposed to die when I was twelve. She had problems with her platelets and ended up in the hospital. The night before she was due to be released, she was found in a pool of blood—she was bleeding out. She was literally dying, and she prayed to God, "Please don't take me now. Wait till my kids can take care of themselves." Miraculously she survived, but it didn't mean she took her medicine regularly or stopped smoking. I didn't know a lot about it— my parents were not the kind of people to tell us exactly what was going on.

It didn't help that I was a selfish teenager, a privileged one who thought she was the shit. There was no talking to me. And I hate myself for it. When I look back now I realized how spoiled we were. My mom and dad made it that I never had to share a room with my brother; then there were the hotels that looked like a castle, and the best steaks when we went out . . . In fact, there was only one time that I saw how hard it was. I found out afterwards that my mom got caught in the store trying to steal some toothpaste for us. I was probably in sixth grade or something. Fortunately, because there were kids in the car, they let her go, but still, I can't imagine what that felt like for her.

My mom had been through so much shit, too. I remember one time, Keith and I were all dressed up one day to get photos taken at Sears, and the three of us went to 7-Eleven afterwards. My mom paid the guy, putting the money in his hand, but when he returned the change, he just rudely dropped it on the counter.

"Did I fucking put the money on the counter when I gave it to you?" my mother shouted. "Put the change in my hand!"

Afterwards, she just referred to him as a white muthafucka. She was not to be played with. I asked her if she was OK.

She just looked at me and smiled. "You know how white folks is," she said.

For a while we'd had to live with my dad's family while he was overseas, too, and that was really hard. But my mom made shit work. And my dad loved her. It was like the TV show *Lovecraft Country*, how the lead couple had to be together because of the pain that they had been through. I really feel like that's what their shit was; I do believe they were in love (one of my uncles confirmed that they were, too). But I also think that at some point it was just friendship. I knew they still had sex, but still I just think that she should have divorced him. I think that she would still be alive if she had.

———————

I wasn't a bad kid, but I was . . . energetic. I was a mischief, a problem child—that's what my mom called me once (hence the name of my first special). I had so much energy . . . But there was more to it.

There are photos of me from back then, and when I look at them now, it stops my heart. In some of those early pictures, there's a light in my smile, a pure, sweet light—innocent, unadulterated, open, trusting. You could tell I was a baby; you could tell I was happy. I can't have been more than one or two . . .

Then, there are photos taken a few years later—probably when I'm three or maybe four years old—and the first and last thing you notice is that light is gone. Completely extinguished. It's just a few years later and there's awareness in those eyes that you can't miss.

What happened to me is still a vivid memory, but it's not something that I let ruin my life. I went through the proper stages of getting my feelings right about what happened back then. But that doesn't mean that it didn't happen or that it didn't affect me. Just look at the photos . . .

Man, I wish I could go back and fight that guy—that little girl couldn't protect herself. That's why I talk to each and every child that comes up to me, giving them love. Because you never know what they're going through.

My parents and I never talked about what had happened in my early childhood—I don't think they knew. Maybe my mom did—she bathed us and I was only two or three years old when it happened—but again, I don't know for sure. My dad definitely didn't know because he would have gotten a murder charge. It was one of my babysitters who messed with me, extinguishing the light in the photographs.

I think if they were alive today, I would certainly tell my parents what happened and how I felt about it.

But honestly, even if there had been a discussion, I'm sure of what my dad would've said to me. He would have been furious, but he would have also been trying to comfort me and trying to make sure I understood to not let that moment define who I am. My dad wasn't the gentlest with his words but we knew he spoke out of love. He definitely would have said, "The world's not going to stop for that shit. This doesn't define who you are. Don't make this the focus of your life. There's always going to be hurt before you get to the right place."

Is that the best advice? Probably not. But I would have been encouraged by it. Parents are supposed to know what they're doing, but now that I'm older, I realize: I would not have known what to do either. Could you imagine finding out that something like that happened to your kid? First of all, having to deal with the devastation of what happened to your child is one thing in and of itself, and then the shame of not stopping it, and then not being able to go to your husband because he'll kill someone.

My daddy didn't play about me. I remember one time, before the abuse, we were in a trailer. It is a very vague memory, but I do remember it was my birthday. I can see the room we were in. It must have been one of the first places I lived, because my brother wasn't born yet. There was a number two candle on the top of a birthday cake. It's chocolate; there's a crowd of people singing "Happy Birthday" to me. I was my dad's kid, and he let me do whatever I wanted with that cake, and that's how I got so much chocolate all over my hands. One of his friends took my hand and put it in his mouth to eat off all the chocolate. I started crying.

My father sees this.

"Don't you ever be touch my daughter, man," he said, plainly.

Then he took that guy outside the trailer, and he beat the shit out of him. I remember the party ended after that. Then my memory stops.

———————

There's another story I really don't want to tell, but I also want to give it to you straight. There was a lot going on with me as a kid—I was being bullied for being dark skinned and loud; I'd been through the abuse; we moved a lot. None of this is an excuse, just an explanation. I was a child.

One day, when I was probably around five years old, I was walking through the trailer park where we lived for a time, and I saw a puppy just lying on the side of the road. I don't know who it belonged to, but for some reason I just started kicking this little puppy, kicking it along the road there. I tell you this because I know that this is a moment in my life when the road split, and I could have gone one of two ways, and the second way was to be a serial killer or even worse.

A woman came running out of her trailer, yelling at me.

"What are you doing?" she screamed. "You're not supposed to do that!" I was so scared, and I knew it was so wrong that I ran—I just ran. I honestly don't know why I'd been doing that to the dog, but I did it.

I think that at the time I thought I'd gotten away with it, but looking back, because of the reaction of that woman from the trailer, I didn't get away with it, in a good way.

I was only a little kid, but I still hate thinking about it today. I get so scared still, for the dog, and for the child.

The psychology of what I was doing is clear: When your power is taken away, you need to reassert it somehow, and what better way than dominating something less powerful than you? I found something more innocent than me and took my agony out on it, and I was trying to regain control because it had been taken away from me.

I'm not trying to explain away what I did—I'm ashamed of it to this day, and it still makes me cry to talk about it—but there's a bigger point than my shame: Parents need to pay close attention to their kids.

I say that because my mom saved my life. I presume that lady told her what she'd seen me doing—thank God. From that point on, my mother started putting me in every activity she could think of. She didn't change toward me at all, but she certainly was watching me much more closely and making sure I just did a ton of stuff. It's not like she had access to counselors; she was just trying to save her child. And she saved me by directing my energy somewhere else.

So, I started sports—football, baseball, softball—and she put me in the choir, and I was a cheerleader. Fuck, I even ended up *teaching* cheerleading.

Eventually the anger in me receded a bit, but then the energy went into a whole different place: I started to try to protect people, whoever I thought was being bullied. I was forever getting in fights because I thought I was protecting them.

It turns out I was stupid. My mom stepped in again.

"You can't be beatin' up people!" she said.

"But I'm protecting them from bullies!" I'd say.

"You *are* the bully," she'd say.

The truth was, I had this chip on my shoulder maybe because of the abuse, or maybe because I was loud and tall and different from everybody else. And, man, if anybody was to touch my brother or my mom . . .

My brother and I were close, but we also fought a lot. Keith was a cute kid, a mama's boy; she loved the shit out of him. But he was also a little fuck. He blackmailed me a lot—a typical brother-sister relationship. I could beat him up, but no one else could. I was very protective of him.

When I was a kid there was a girl who had been picking on my brother regularly, and one time I saw her actually push him. The next thing I can remember is hearing my brother's voice, far away, as if through water, "Leslie, please stop! You going to kill her."

When I came to, I was choking her. All I remember thinking was *I have to eliminate the problem*. Another time, my brother went missing, and I was beside myself, hysterical; I was scared that someone was abusing him like I'd been abused . . . My parents had to calm me down. It turned out he was just at football practice and hadn't told anyone.

I was like that about protecting my mom, too.

Friday night was fun night at home—we'd always go to Pizza Hut and get two pizzas for $10.99 then watch a movie. One night when we arrived home, my mom found onions on her pizza. She hated onions on a pizza, so we went back to the store.

There, she was trying to explain to the guy behind the counter about the onions, but he kept interrupting her. He was a pimply white teenager; he seemed to be stressed by how busy they were that night, and started yelling at my mother.

"I ordered one pizza with onions and the other without—" my mother started.

"There are no onions on this pizza," he said.

"Oh no, there's onions all over—" my mom started to say.

"Where?" he shouted. "Right there? Right there? Right there?" while he poked into the pizza with his pimply little fingers.

I.

Blacked.

Out.

For the next few moments all I could hear, as though through a distant megaphone, far, far away, was someone yelling "Leslie! Leslie, baby! Leslie!"

Apparently, I had jumped over the counter and grabbed that muthafucka by the throat. I was only in the twelfth grade, but I was big. I'm told I was screaming, "Muthafucka, don't you ever talk to my mama like that. You say you're sorry, muthafucka," over and over, while my mom shouted, "Leslie! Leslie, baby! Leslie!" I can still hear the fear for me in her voice.

The manager finally appeared, and I let the guy go. The manager then apologized that his employee had been so rude to my mom (she was a regular), and we got two brand-new pizzas. On the way home in the car my mom just kept saying, "Girl? Girl!?"

"Ma, you can't talk to my mama like that," I said. "That's just some bullshit."

"You're as strong as a muthafucka," she said with awe in her voice.

At home Mom told my dad what I'd done, and he laughed with pride.

"Goddamn right, muthafucka," my dad said. "I would have fucked him up, too."

———————

By the way, I wasn't always beating people up—there was a flip side to my personality. As early as fifth and sixth grade, I realized there was some funny shit about me, so I naturally became the class clown. That got me in trouble, too.

I had a best friend in fifth and sixth grade we used to call Rerun, because he looked just like Freddy "Rerun" Stubbs from *What's Happening!!* But my friend Rerun wasn't much of a best friend—he was always getting me in shit.

In fifth grade, *Good Times* was as popular as *What's Happening!!*, so it wasn't much of a stretch to refer to my teacher in the same way that James, Willona, and J.J. referred to the building superintendent, only I added the word *head* to the end to be creative.

The teacher was onto me about something one day, and that's when I referred to her as "Buffalo Butthead" to Rerun.

Bad idea. Rerun told on me immediately.

That poor teacher—she cried in front of everybody when she heard that, and I remember thinking, *Oh, I done fucked up . . .* She sent me to talk to the principal. When he asked me what I'd done, I told him I'd called somebody a name.

"You can't be calling people names," he said.

I looked down at the floor.

"What did you call the teacher?"

"I called her . . . Buffalo Butthead."

"Oh no, no, no!" he yelled. Everyone knew who "Buffalo Butt" was back then. "That's so wrong. You can't be calling people 'Buffalo Butthead.' I was going to let you off with a scolding, but now you gotta go on home."

So, I did, and when I told my mom why I'd been sent home, boy did my mom beat my ass. When she was done, she said, "Listen to me—you're going to go to that school tomorrow and you going to fucking apologize to her," and I was thinking, *That's fine, I'll just lie and say that I did it.* But I swear she could read my mind. My mom would always say, "You can't hustle a hustler. I know what you're doing." She knew I wasn't going to do what I said I'd do. She wasn't stupid; she knew her kid was crazy.

"And I know you're going to apologize because I'm going to call her and I'm going to ask her if you apologized."

Shit . . .

Next day at school after class, sure enough I went up to the teacher's desk. I did not want to do this. But part of me was concerned that I'd hurt her feelings and I knew she'd make a big deal of my apology. I didn't want to deal with these big emotions at that age. I was always having to apologize for some shit.

"I'm sorry for calling you Buffalo Butthead," I said.

Then, she did exactly what I was afraid of—that teacher extracted the very worst punishment you can imagine for a nine-year-old: She made me kiss her cheek. No one has ever moved faster than me running out of that classroom that day.

You think I'd have learned my lesson, having to kiss a teacher, but in sixth grade I went one better.

Once again it was Rerun's fault.

My teacher in sixth grade was Mrs. Buck, a short old white lady who always wore a turtleneck. She was actually a really sweet lady, but you know . . . kids vs. teachers . . . One day, she made me move away from Rerun because we were making too much noise or something. I was so mad at her for that, so I wrote "Miss Buck is an asshole" on a little strip of paper and stashed it in my desk.

Rerun must have had some secret hate against me. He found the piece of paper and put it on Mrs. Buck's desk.

I was dying inside. I watched her read it, and tears started to form in her eyes.

"Who wrote this?" she said in her squeaky old-lady voice. But she was looking right at me—she knew I was probably the only kid in the class who would write some dumb shit like that.

"Did you?" she said, pointing at me.

Then, everybody was looking at me, because they all knew it could only be me, too.

"You know what?" she said, her voice shaking. "I'm a good teacher. And I really try . . ." And with that, she walked outside into the hallway, and we could all hear her sobbing.

All this happened right before juice and snacks. The whole class turned around and looked at me.

"Yo, bitch, if you've fucked up the juice and snacks, we going to whoop your ass," someone said to a murmur of agreement from everyone else. "So, you take your ass out there and make this right."

Aw man, fuck, the class is mad at me.

Sure enough, I got up and went outside. I was taller than Mrs. Buck already, but I truly felt smaller right then as she stood there, tears streaming down her face.

"Mrs. Buck, I am so sorry," I said, "I was just so mad that you moved me, but that's no reason for me to be writing something so terrible."

Mrs. Buck's tears stopped, and she brightened a bit. But I felt she needed one more word of explanation.

"And I just learned how to spell 'asshole,'" I said, "so I wanted to write it on a piece of paper."

Basically, I was saying that it was her fault for being a good teacher and teaching me how to spell.

"You. Are. Just. Too. Much," Mrs. Buck said, laughing. Then, she hugged me.

"Can I go get the juice and cookies now?" I said, maybe pushing my luck.

"Yes," she said, "you can go get the juice and cookies."

Later that year, we had a parade, and we made a float of Hansel and Gretel. The whole class voted me to be the Witch. I was devastated—I cried and cried and cried. *Why does my class think I'm a witch?* I cried all the way home and when my mom asked me what was going on I told her.

"So, you're the witch, huh?" she said. "Well, don't you know that the witch is the star of the show?" Then she proceeded to tell me the whole story of Hansel and Gretel, how the witch is a bomb role, like one of the main characters, and made me an amazing outfit from material she had lying around—half dark blue, half light blue—and a witch's hat and handed me her broom.

We'd built a whole house on the float and everything, and on the day of the parade I was flying around, shouting *"Wooo! Waaah! Wooo!"* I think I got the bug back then, seeing everyone laughing at me and scaring all the little ones. And we won! And it was all because of me, the Witch.

I was starting to realize even then that I liked an audience and knew how to get a reaction out of people. I figured I could translate this into anything I did, so when I heard that we were putting on a play about Christopher Columbus—who back then was still the shit—I headed straight to an audition for the lead singing role of Queen Isabella. I knew she had a solo, and having killed with my Witch performance, I figured I could kill once again as Queen Izzy.

I practiced that muthafuckin' solo for weeks, singing every night in my room, and sending my mom and dad and little brother nuts.

And then it was the day of the auditions.

The girl ahead of me seemed to think she was a diva or something, wailing away in a flute-y soprano, but when I heard how *she* was singing, I was not to be outdone. I strode into that audition and let them have it—*Bitch,* I thought, *you're not the only one who can sing some opera*:

> *When a man has a dream*
> *Who would ever dare to tear them apart?*

(And I can still sing that shit, every note, to this day.)

I wish I could paint a portrait of the faces of the people in that room. First they froze, then the frowning started, then people did that one-eye thing when you hit the wrong notes and pain became etched across their entire faces.

I was trying to be an opera singer, but I'd never seen or even heard an opera, so it turned out to simply be a very bad imitation of Mary Poppins—I wasn't so much singing as calling back the dead. The notes were very high, but with no relation to music ever heard by human beings. Even dogs were like, "Yo! Shut up!"

I got a role, though: one of Queen Isabella's maidens. It was less of a singing role. Actually, it was a non-singing role. I just stood there during the play doing nothing, in my long white Easter dress—which was my costume—watching the back of the head of this opera girl, thinking, *Oh, one day, bitches, one day . . .*

Because now I really had the bug.

———————

So yeah, I loved an audience from early on. When we lived on the base at Fort Bragg, a bunch of us kids used to have skateboard shows—I had this see-through orange fiberglass skateboard that I would show off and do tricks on. (I was actually really good.)

My father's postings meant that we moved around a lot—Fort Bragg, North Carolina, then back to Memphis. Then he'd be gone again—Korea, I guess?

We were thriving as a family in North Carolina. We had a house in College Downs, but I tore the bathroom up. I thought I was Nadia Comăneci. I had tried out for the gymnastics team, but I was told I was too tall. So, I was taking a shower one day, and I figured I'd swing on the bar that holds the shower curtain. Back then the rods were often ceramic—muthafucka held me for two swings before it came crashing down.

There I was, on the floor, butt naked, surrounded by crushed ceramics and bits of plaster from the walls. When my mom heard the crash, she rushed to the bathroom. I tried to pretend I was hurt, but she saw right through it, and beat my ass.

"And your daddy is going to beat your ass when he gets home," she said.

But that night, when my dad heard what had happened, he came into my bedroom, closed the door, and started to howl with laughter.

"The whole bathroom, huh?" he said.

That's when I think they started to realize I was crazy . . . and funny.

"We might have to get that girl some help," he said to my mom later.

———————

After Fort Bragg we moved to Memphis—we were a family there, as Dad was around a lot more.

Then Dad worked for a radio station, using his experience as electronic engineer for the legendary WDIA in Memphis. WDIA was the first station aimed directly at Black Americans—B.B. King once worked there, and it's said that Elvis listened to WDIA and was influenced by what he heard. It was the first station to hire a Black DJ, too, and it's reckoned that at one point the signal reached 10 percent of all Black Americans, from Missouri to Florida.

WDIA is the most famous radio station in Memphis, and Dad drove the WDIA van, so he thought he was a little celebrity. He'd drop me off at school in that van, rolling up with the music blasting. This made him *the* most popular person—made us *all* the most popular. We went to a ton of concerts, too, and because he was a DJ, I got heavily into music (I still am). When it comes to music, it's as if my dad took a piece of his soul and poured it into me. (Later in California, when I went to parties as a teenager, I'd have all the albums, so when I had to go home, that was when the party ended.)

My brother acclimated well to the move to Memphis, but in grade school and middle school I was still fighting everyone on the street because when you're the tallest, other kids will haze you to see if you were cool enough to take it. Dad's job at the radio station meant I eventually became popular, though. I'd worked hard to make a bunch of good friends in Memphis. One, Kandace Thomas, was my best friend, and in Georgian Hills Junior High, even though we were kinda the nerds, we also managed to be thought of as the cool kids, somehow, too, and people liked me because I was funny.

We worked for that popularity. We were friends with the finest boys in school: Rodney Boyd, Michael Boyd (no relation), Larry Jackson (all his brothers were fine actually), and Larry Granderson. (If I quantum leapt back now, I'd probably just think they were straight nerds.)

We ran the first ever catfish, too. We wanted to become popular with Rodney and Michael and the two Larrys, so we got a picture of Kandace's cousin, a beautiful girl with curly hair. Now, looking back, she looked a bit like Ola Ray. The cousin went to a whole different school—that's how we were able to pull this whole thing off. I called Michael Boyd, pretending to be the cousin, and told him that Leslie and Kandace were "my best friends;" Kandace was calling Larry Jackson and doing the same thing. So when we got to school, the hot boys wanted to be friends with us because they liked the girl, as she was apparently friends with us. The plan was supposed to be that the cousin was going to come to our Friday night dance, but she got in trouble and got put on punishment, and never showed up. Eventually the whole thing fell apart anyway when we finally met the girl at a track meet, and realized that she had a tooth missing. But by then those fine boys became our friends, so it didn't matter.

We didn't know what it was going to be like at high school, though, because there's always a recalibration of friendships and who's cool and who's not between junior high and high school, but at Trezevant, the school everyone wanted to go to in Memphis, I managed to snag a spot in the marching band—which is like being a jock—in my first week. This was a huge deal; this meant I would be instantly popular. My dad had taught me to twirl rifles, so that's what I did for the audition—I think I got the spot because I managed to not hit myself in the head with the rifle (or shoot anyone, even though they were fake plastic guns).

Me and Kandace were going to run Trezevant High School. And then my dad came home at the end of that first week and announced we were moving to California. He said he'd gotten a job working at Stevie Wonder's radio station.

Stevie had met my dad at a concert—he was always at gigs—and loved him. My dad was on a mission to get us the fuck out of Memphis. He wanted to be a player in the Hollywood game, and he knew he couldn't be one in Tennessee, so this was perfect for him. He'd always wanted to be in show business; he loved music.

It wasn't perfect for me. I burst into tears; I was devastated.

"You're ruining my life," I said. Just when I'd become popular and was ready to rule high school, here we were moving again, this time all the way across the country to California.

Chapter Two

JUMP STUPID

"**Y**ou going to love California," my dad had said. Stevie Wonder had picked Dad to help him at his radio station, the legendary KJLH. Stevie had created a motto to match the call sign: "Kindness, joy, love, and happiness," but to me, this move west wasn't kind, it wasn't joyful, and it didn't make me happy. And I most certainly did not love it.

No, I thought, *this is the end of my life.* I was going from Memphis, where I finally felt at home and was popular, to Los Angeles, where I would know no one.

Initially, we moved into the good part of Lynwood in South LA, and rented my uncle's house, so our living situation was cool, but it was a culture shock. I was a country-ass bitch in this elevated place. I had never met girls like this; I had never met boys like this. They wore shorts to school? Like what the fuck am I dealing with? I can do that, too?

OK then, I will: First day of school, I wore my shorts. I remember exactly what I had on: blue shorts with this red line down the side, a red Izod shirt, and tennis shoes. I thought I was the shit, but I soon learned that I had on both the gang colors, so, er, that's a problem.

"So, you got on the red shirt and blue shorts, huh?" someone said. "You obviously not from here."

"Yeah, I just moved here," I said. I thought I was talking regular, but apparently it was clear to everyone in LA that I was talking "country."

"Where you from?" someone else said.

"Tennessee."

"That's what we going to call you, then," and they did.

———————

Soon after we moved to California, I came out of my room one night. My dad was lying on the couch, a little buzzed. He noticed my long face, and he sat up.

"What's wrong with you?" he said.

I looked at him.

"Daddy," I said, "do you think I'm pretty?"

He looked like he didn't understand the question.

"Pretty?" he said. "You are the most beautiful girl I've ever seen in my life. Are you kidding me? What? What's wrong with you? You're beautiful."

"For real?"

"Yeah, for real. You're my daughter. Of course you're pretty."

And I remember thinking, *OK then, fuck everybody else.*

And I still think that to this day.

At first, I hated the nickname Tennessee, but when the cool guys called me it, I was fine with it. And despite wearing both gang colors that first day, I knew I already had one big advantage: I was tall, so I knew they'd respect me when they saw me play basketball, because I'd been on the team in Georgia Hills.

At the tryout, though, I was horrified to find out that these bitches could play, too. Shit!

I was so green.

Coach Van Girard from the varsity team told Coach Buggs of the JV team, "She's strong. She's tall. She can do a layup. And she's willing to learn. We can mold that. But we need to get her some shoes—those cloth Converse won't do it."

I realized that I had to become a jock to be popular, and I think they could see that drive in me. I could jump out the gym, and I wanted to be good. I wasn't scared to block shots. I didn't have the right shoes, but I'd shown up to play.

I got good so fast that I only spent maybe a half of a semester on the JV team before I got put on the varsity squad. And that was a good team! They made the playoffs ten straight years under Van Girard, and even won the California Interscholastic Federation tournament in 1986, which is a big deal. But I thought about what my dad said: As long as I worked hard, it didn't matter. Basketball hadn't even been my main sport before that. I'd done all the sports, but with basketball I'd found my lane, plus my dad really loved basketball. It wasn't like I loved it, but I was tall, strong, tough, and aggressive, and I worked hard. That was enough to get me on that team as a starter.

But at home, the family had started to splinter. I was a teenager now; my brother had started getting wilder friends. My mom was trying to keep us all ahead, going to church on Sundays, doing everything she could to hold the family together. Who the fuck knows what my dad was doing? We were all in our own worlds.

In California, my brother was way more popular than me. (I was tall, dorky, country.) He loved me, and I loved him, but by this point we were more like roommates than close siblings. He and I would come together for family stuff, but once he got caught stealing the first time in LA, when he was about twelve, things really changed.

Keith had stolen video games from a discount retail store called Zodys. The police came, and my mom handled it.

"Please don't tell Daddy," Keith said.

"I have to," she said. "That's your father, my husband. I can't keep nothing like that from him."

Dad didn't whoop him when he found out, but even so, Keith knew he'd fucked up. Dad was listening to music that night; that's when we knew he was stressed about something. My brother went in to talk to him.

"Daddy, I'm so sorry," my brother sobbed.

"I'm just really disappointed in you, son."

This broke my brother.

After that, Dad just stopped bothering to discipline him—and little by little the problems elevated. Keith had a ton of peer pressure on him, too, and I felt so sorry for him. Kids just stole back then; I thought, *How the fuck did you get caught?*

———————

About three years into our time in California I started to notice that every time a name got mentioned—JB Stone, I'll never forget it—my mom would roll her eyes. He was a colleague of my dad at Stevie Wonder's radio station, and eventually I found out why Mom seemed so pissed about him: something happened and JB Stone got demoted . . . but my dad got fired. We'd come all the way away from Memphis for this, and now it was gone. I never found out exactly what happened, but without that job, we couldn't stay in the nice part of Lynwood, so we moved to the tough part.

"Everything's going to be fine," Dad said. But everything wasn't fine. There was way more stress in the house. Money was tight (though there wasn't much I wanted for, to be honest).

My mom still had her ailments, but I didn't really know much about what was happening with that. Parents were shadowy figures then; they didn't share everything with their kids, like now. And anyway, a kind of teenage selfishness was coming over me.

I was just turning senior when Dad lost his gig with Stevie, and I had a total tantrum. It was the only time I had a tantrum. We're gonna be in the hood, now.

"We're not going to have any money!" I shouted. "I want to go to the prom and stuff, and you're not going to have money now—it's fucked up. This is my senior year. I'm not going to be able to get my class ring."

My dad just said, "Don't worry about it," but to a rising senior, this was a disaster. Dad started a business installing speakers and sound systems, but I knew things weren't going well because my mom was working her butt off at the cable company just to keep us afloat.

———————

To add to my family's stress, we were now in a tougher part of Lynwood in the 1980s during the height of the crack era.

In the meantime, basketball was my savior. I was going to go to college to play, and then I was going to go overseas and play. I was going to be a professional basketball player, and then I was going to be the first Black woman to play in the NBA. Those were my dreams, but I was the most inconsistent fucking player ever. I was really good—just not every time I played.

But let me tell you something—the beginning of my senior year? We had a ton of tournaments, and I was playing like I was possessed, because my dad had lost his job, and I knew the only way I'd get to college was to get a scholarship.

After every game Coach Girard would basically be in tears because he would be both exhilarated and frustrated.

"I don't know what your formula is!" he'd say. "I don't know how to make you do this. You just do it when you want to. But that doesn't work! I need you to do it when I need you to do it. I can scream at you till I'm blue in the face, but if you don't have the passion it won't happen." You've got to learn to play like you practice. That's true for anything in your life!

I wanted it to turn it on, too, but the truth was, even though I was good at it, I didn't really like playing basketball! It was a means to an end. (I wouldn't have been able to describe it like that then.) Even when I wanted to play better, I couldn't automatically play well; I didn't know what it was that shifted. The one thing I carry from that to this day is that it's all about *passion*. You have to *want* to do something. And I didn't have passion for basketball.

Coach Girard realized though that I played hard when I was pissed off, so before each game, he would make me mad, so that I'd play crazy.

Sometimes Coach would let us leave our books in his classroom to save us carrying them across campus—but then to make me mad, he'd say we had to take our book bags with us, and those things were heavy, and it was a long-ass walk to our lockers. Or he would suddenly decide that he wouldn't give me a hall pass but give one to someone else. Anything he could do to piss me off.

And I don't know how, but I fell for it every time.

And then? I would *destroy*. That's when Girard started calling me "Chocolate Thunder."

The nickname Tennessee was cute, but Chocolate Thunder got respect. During one practice we were fucking around, and I was palming the ball and showing off, and someone was flickering the lights and announcing me as Chocolate Thunder. (Darryl Dawkins, the original Chocolate Thunder, got that nickname from Stevie Wonder, of all people.) I was a showman even then.

I started getting scouted, too, all these scouts from colleges showing up on the Lynwood High School campus for me—it was a big thing. One of them, Coach Brian Berger from Chapman College in Orange, California, reminded me of my dad, because he was very strict. Dad had always told us to have our asses in the house before the streetlights come on. There was no missing school; if we got bad grades, we didn't get new sneakers. Berger had that same kind of approach to discipline.

I also think I liked Coach because he liked me. He would smile at the shit I did; he understood me. (Sometimes he hated the showboating, but he loved it when I lost it.) During one game, Coach Berger was in the stands, and I was playing my ass off. I was getting steals, blocking shots, everything. At one point there was a rebound that I dove for, grabbed, and threw to the guard, who made the two. I jumped up and I screamed in a showboaty way, "What the fuck? What the fuck? Yea-ah!"

When I looked over at Coach Berger, he was beaming. He liked that shit? Oh, I gotta go play for him.

———————

I don't remember meeting my friend Faye Sherrod; it felt like she was just always there. She was always on my side, and she knew all the fun things to do; she got me to skip school, and I never did that. She knew all the gangsters, too.

Faye is still my friend. Back then we were the same height, and she was beautiful. Whenever she would play, her titties would move around and everybody would shout, "Look at Faye's big-ass titties!"

It was great being around Faye; she was so positive, so sunny. She always had a smile on her face, even when she got in trouble. Coach would yell, "Stop smiling!" but she just couldn't help it. (Our other friend Lynn only made things worse by pop-locking behind Coach as he shouted.) I loved hanging out with Faye, but you never really knew where she would be at—she seldom came to school. And even though she was such a happy person, that didn't stop her joining me in fighting everybody. Faye would shout, "Fuck them bitches!" with a huge smile on her face. She was a great player, too, and tough, and if we were on the court at the same time, we would sometimes do something called "jump stupid." We'd surround a bitch, walk around her menacingly, shouting, "What you going to do? Are you going jump stupid? You ain't going to do nothing. Jump stupid jump stupid . . ."

Which basically means if you feel froggish, bitch, leap!

I was a dirty player—oh God, I was so dirty. That was my thing: I was the intimidator. But our games were just rough generally—I would hurt so many people, often on purpose. I would foul out, sometimes in the first half, just to make a point. I would go over to the other team at the beginning of the game, and I would say, "I have five fouls, bitches . . . I got five of them."

Or during the game I'd say, "Don't bring your ass in my house," and then, once I'd fouled out, I would sit on the bench and if someone even looked like they were going into the key, I would yell, "Don't go in my house!"

And they wouldn't—I trained them with my intimidation.

I could score, no problem, but my whole thing was defense; I was like Rodman, banging off the boards, grabbing rebounds, elbows up.

Actually, I was more like Bill Laimbeer.

But despite making my way on the basketball court, I still got made fun of a lot, bullied by some of my peer teammates (the seniors didn't give a fuck). And it wasn't physical bullying—it was mental. I could fight any one of those bitches on the team, but fighting them wasn't the thing to do; I saved that for opposing teams. Besides, if I fought them they would know they were getting to me.

I would complain to Coach Girard: "You never say nothing to these bitches. You never tell them to leave me the fuck alone. And you see them fucking with me."

He'd just say, "You're fine." I'm sure he was used to teenage drama, especially with teenaged girls, but sometimes I wish he would have said more.

Beyond Faye and Lynn, I didn't want to be like the other girls on the team. I wanted to be Leslie Fucking Jones, even if I didn't fully know who that was yet.

I knew in my head that I was better than them, but I didn't know how to be better, if that makes sense.

For some reason—and it's hard to explain this one—I didn't really know what I was, or who I was, even down to sometimes wearing my brother's clothes because they fit me. I didn't know how to dress in a feminine way; my mom was always working but she still did everything she could; I just wanted to blend into the background. Yes, I was an athlete, but there were a lot of things about me that I didn't really understand. I knew that I was growing; I knew that maybe I was becoming my own person. Maybe I was just a loner? And I'd been through a lot: the constant moving, the family stuff, what happened to me early in life. I wasn't a victim, but I was confused.

It is very frustrating to be around people who you think don't like you or are talking about you. I made a lot of mistakes, and sometimes I think I fucked up practice on purpose just to make us all have to run to get back at the teammates who bullied me (I didn't care about running). And whenever we had to run because of me, the team would get so mad. So much so that one night one of my teammates, the girl who bullied me the most—I'm not going to use her name because she's not worth it, so we'll just call her "This Bitch"—had been made to drive me home after practice, but she just left me at school because I'd made everyone have to run.

It was nighttime in Lynwood. Everyone had gone home, and I was left to walk those streets alone. I knew I'd be fine because I knew my hood, but still, "This Bitch" made me walk home after practice in the dark. It was fucked up, plain and simple, because she was supposed to be the person who got me home. I was still only sixteen years old, and you never knew when your hood might turn on a girl alone. And forget all that: This shit was supposed to be taken care of! The only reason my mom even let me stay late to do those practices was because I would get a ride home and not be left to fend for myself. "This Bitch" had let me down in every possible way. (Coach Girard was pissed, too, when he heard about it later—he knew he would have been the first call if anything had happened to me.)

Next day I overheard her bragging about leaving me. I decided to take action—I was done with this bullying shit. At lunchtime, I went straight up to "This Bitch."

"Yo," I said, "why the fuck did you leave me? That's fucked up."

"This Bitch" just started talking shit, talking and talking, like I don't get a say, like she didn't care that she'd left me to walk home, like the bullying would never end, so I decided to change that situation. I grabbed her, shoved her through the door, then out in the hallway. I held her tightly and said, "I'm tired of this shit, so it's time for you to die. You have pushed me too far. Y'all think I'm a punk. I'm not a punk. I just don't give you energy. But since you want to play this game, I'm going to show you exactly how strong I am."

And with that I physically picked her up.

"I'm going to throw you off the fucking floor," I said, as though I was going to hurl her off the second floor of the B Building.

By this point, "This Bitch" is screaming, until my Samoan friend, Big Tina, stopped me. Even Coach Girard grabbed me before I got to the railing.

Actually, I'm not even sure it happened exactly that way. But Big Tina real.

"This Bitch" never left me after practice again. I always got a ride after that. And I never got benched for that shit—I was just too good to be left out of the game.

———————

Morningside, Dominguez Hills, Compton—if we were beating those rival schools, the driver would have the bus running before the end of the game. The kids from those schools would shake the bus as we drove away; once in a while they'd even throw bricks at it.

Compton was the worst—even I was scared when we had to play them. They were the next town over, so this was the biggest possible rivalry, especially since the summer before, when I'd hurt one of Compton's players during a game.

When we played them during the summers, they would punk all our players, except for me. If they even looked like they were considering it, I'd say, "Fuck you, bitch, I live in Lynwood. I know all the gangsters. Fuck all y'all." And that would do the trick.

But still, they had some girls who were intimidating— even I'd think, *Nah, I'm not going to fight her.*

Then, we had to play them in a championship game. It was the furthest Lynwood High School had ever gotten, and now it was just Compton in the way of us making regionals.

Just about everyone was at this game—my dad didn't go, and Mom couldn't because she had to work, even though she really wanted to—but everybody else was at this game. Even people who didn't go to Lynwood anymore showed up. The place was packed. Even a young Suge Knight was there. (Yes—I went to high school with Marion Knight.)

There was one dude in particular, specifically, who I was happy to see show up—Philip. I was so in love with Philip—big crush! He was definitely out of school by then. He had a Jheri curl and everything.

It was clear to everyone from the outset: The only way we were going to win this game was if I, Chocolate Thunder, brought it. But I was scared man, because just like everybody else, I wasn't sure what I needed to do to turn that passion on. I didn't know how to make myself perform to my highest potential. I needed to find that place where it's "bitch, go." To this day I can get myself to that place. It comes to me when I'm just waking up from a nap or on the road to a gig, or when I'm about to start a set or I've just come offstage from a show, or backstage at a TV taping, or driving my dope-ass BMW through Los Angeles. When I close my eyes, I can see myself walking through a field of flowers, just free, letting myself go, not allowing anything to hold me back, fully myself. When it happens onstage, I can make everything disappear and just perform. It's a feeling of pure freedom; no judgment: *Just do you. Go.*

Flashes of that night of the game against Compton come to me now: I remember having on a headband . . . and I remember being scared . . . but I also remember being over it, and something else kicked in: A mindset came over me that I was just going to do it. That night against Compton was one of the first times I was able to conjure up that feeling and use it.

More flashes of memory come: I was sitting on the bench . . . and then I remember us warming up . . . and the mass of people in the bleachers . . . and Philip . . . and Compton were showing their asses, and jumping in our faces . . . and then suddenly—and I don't know how—something switched in my brain, and the game was running, and I started jumping back. I remember one bitch was trying to scare me—she was specifically coming after me, and she was scoring. And in my head, I was saying, *OK, let's get her out the game. You wanna come after me bitch? Come after me.* From then on, every time she looked like she was about to do something, I would be right up on her. I was getting all the rebounds and I was doing my scoring, but I also started to be able to stop her from scoring.

Then, quick as you like, that bitch got four fouls. Then she couldn't fuck with me. But now I wanted more—I wanted her out of the game so I could take over. It was on me, all me. Then, she came down from a rebound, I went right up under, she landed on me, and I flailed around as though I was hurt.

Foul number five. She was gone.

People are now on their feet; I can see Philip on his feet, screaming "Leslie!" And I thought, *Oh, I must be doing good.*

We beat Compton by five or ten points that night, I forget how many. I wish my dad had seen it, and my mom, but they were working. But what was most important was how I'd been able to conjure up that focus, that drive, that strength. This wasn't just basketball anymore.

In the regionals, we came up against Locke High School from South LA near Watts. Have you ever seen those movies where a team is all ready to play and the other team shows up and they're giants? One huge player for Locke in particular stood out: Doretha Caldwell. I don't even think she spoke; I seem to remember she just growled. Locke beat us, and that was that—but now I had to pick a college.

Coach Berger came to my house to offer me a scholarship to Chapman. I was so proud. I was going to get the fuck out of the house, and it was going to pay for college. And I remember vividly that he asked me, "Is there anything that you want?"

I now wish I'd said, "Do not bring 'This Bitch' to your school." Yup, sure enough, "This Bitch" had gotten an offer to Chapman, too, and would be following me to college to torture me even more.

That's one thing I would have changed for sure—I would have *insisted* "This Bitch" didn't go to school with me. But I didn't. I still wasn't sure who I was or what I could get out of life, so I just let it go. I wish I hadn't; I would never do anything like that now, trust. I'd throw a bitch off a balcony before not asserting myself.

Meanwhile, at home, Mom was still working long hours at the cable company on Long Beach Boulevard to keep us fed. At one point, HBO was about to air a Tina Turner concert, and the cable company was responsible for doing the promotion. It fell to my mom to put an event together, and she did an amazing job. She put out black and gold on the tables, hung silk curtains . . . it was so beautiful. I remember walking in and saying, "Ma, you did this? Oh my God!" This is the proudest I ever felt of my mom. And I think she was very proud of herself, too. It's one time that she got to really do something that she put together herself, and it was beautiful. She loved that job because she liked the people she worked with, and they loved her back. Mom was there until she got sick and she wasn't going to get any better.

Chapter Three

COACH BERGER

After high school I headed to Chapman University in Orange County. I was a jock, no question. And I loved playing for Coach Berger. He was a great coach—even then he was being recruited by Division 1 schools. But he had stayed at Chapman because he had always lived in Orange County—that's where he'd met his wife, and they'd raised their family there, too.

But after I'd played for him for a year, Coach Berger got fired. Our star player, Leone Patterson, played her ass off one year, and Berger sent an article about Leone to another school's athletic director saying they should go fuck themselves, something like that. When Chapman found out, they fired him on the spot. But it didn't matter—Colorado State recruited him almost immediately.

Coach Berger had been strict, but I liked that—it reminded me of my dad, as I've said. His mustache was straight and full, like a cowboy—you never saw his top lip. He was very 1987. His eyes were calm like the water that flowed through his backyard—beautiful pools, light and peaceful and deep blue. (Yes, he had a creek that ran through his backyard—what is the purpose of that creek? Is that where he gets his water? Does he fish there? How white do you have to be to have a creek in your backyard?) He was a beautiful man and would have made a perfect sheriff.

The *Los Angeles Times* ran a piece about him when he was my coach, and this is what they wrote (and it's a *perfect* description of him): "[He has] a face that at one moment can show mild contempt for a person and the next breaks up in laughter. His eyes, steely in composition, have been known to freeze a player at 20 paces. Combine it all with a thick black mustache, and you have Wyatt Earp in a sweat suit." That's right—Wyatt Earp in a sweat suit. And listen, you did what Berger said because Coach knew what he was talking about. And if we fucked up, he made us run—man, did he make us run. I had to run thirty suicides for every class I missed. Problem was, I missed ten classes once, and he made me run every one of those three hundred suicides. He was not to be played with. Berger didn't give a fuck; it didn't matter if we were missing dinner—those were just the consequences. Berger even made the assistant coach watch me run them, too, just in case I decided to cheat. Coach did not fuck around.

To even make the team, you first had to do thirty suicides, and each suicide had to be finished in thirty-three seconds or less. You couldn't join the team until you nailed it.

Man, I was so healthy back then; my body was hard, and hot! I was a machine. But Berger said that me and my friend, Valerie Hartsfield, were too muscle-bound. We'd been friends since our second day at school; we'd been there in August before school started. Val had guns, and big calves because she had a sweet jump shot, and I was strong, too, but we were just heavy from all our muscle. Coach Berger just wanted us lean; if we were going to be the best we could be, we had to have peak endurance, the strongest possible stamina, and be *all* muscle.

"I need you to be able to keep up with these guards," Berger told the team, "so you need to get in shape. That's why y'all are going to be running those suicides."

Neither me nor Val made the suicides the first time, so he made us do our next set together.

We were fine for the first twenty—well, not fine, we were actually cursing out everyone and their muthafuckin' mamas. But we were getting them done in around twenty-seven seconds, which was good . . . until we got to the twenty-sixth. I was delirious.

By then, Berger, the assistant coach, and the entire team were watching. Someone said, "This is fucking wonderful and beautiful."

We didn't think so. Val and I were cheering each other on—"Come on, bitch! You can do it, bitch! We got this shit, bitch!"—(Coach Berger couldn't understand why we called each other bitch)—and everyone else was yelling at us, too, because they knew we were good and wanted us to make the team. I just needed to make the team because they could take my scholarship away if I didn't. (Looking back, he might have given me a second chance, but I didn't know that at the time.)

"We're going do this, bitch. Fuck this!" I screamed. Each thirty seconds of rest between each suicide run felt like a single second in time.

"Fuck these muthafuckas," Val yelled, "we got this shit."

White people ain't seen that much cursing, trust, not that way. These two sisters screaming "Fuck this!" and running back and forth. I looked over at Coach Berger—I swear he had this expression on his face as though he was thinking, *These chicks are like gladiators.*

Everybody was so hyped. Twenty-seven turned into twenty-eight turned into twenty-nine. The entire team is now yelling at us: "Bitch you're going to do this. Go, bitch, go, fucking go!" By number thirty, I was ready to die. Like, dead die. I was heaving and praying, "Oh God, I'm going to die, please, Jesus, kill me. *Goddddd! Nooooo! Jesuss!!!! Fuck this shit!!!!!*"

Running the shit out of us really brought Coach Berger joy. (I once got my tooth knocked out during practice. He told me to just push it back into place and keep going.)

And then it was over, and we'd done it, and we'd made the team. The place was going crazy, and we all went out and got hammered together. (It was the first time I'd ever gotten drunk. We ended up hanging out with the water polo team. Right before I passed out, I remember asking one of them,

"How do y'all get the horses in the water?") But there was a real, genius point to all this: now, the team was as one, all pulling in the right direction, and we took that camaraderie into actual games.

That is, until we played Northern Arizona twice in Arizona.

We lost the first game, when we shouldn't have lost either of them—we were clearly better than they were.

For a start, we had Leone Patterson.

Leone was from New Zealand; six foot, a forward, she was a Kodak first team All-American and CCAA player of the year, and would eventually go on to be the leading scorer in conference history.

I had been the bruiser in my high school, and I'd never been scared of a white girl, ever, never, ever, until the first time I had to guard Leone Patterson in a scrimmage. Everybody was talking about how good she was. I was like, "Whatever, bitch, this white bitch ain't going to do shit." Then *blam!* Her elbows up, she came right into me.

"Bitch!" I screamed. "You can't do that."

Turns out she could, and did, and nothing was going to stop her. She had this attacking position where her elbows never went down—they were like knives. So, if she had the ball and she was coming towards you, she was going to fuck you up.

Leone didn't talk to anybody, either—she didn't give a shit about all the bullshit that other college kids cared about. If what you were saying didn't have something to do with basketball, she just ignored it. She didn't party, or anything—she just kept those elbows up and scored hundreds of points. I was scared of her, but also inspired.

Leone taught me something so valuable about how to play. One day she looked at how I stood and said in her New Zealand accent (I once said, "You sound like Crocodile Dundee," and she just growled and said, *"Auck!* I'm not from Australia. I'm from New Zealand—they're not the fucking same!"), "You just need to get lower when you're defending, you have more power that way. There's a time you can keep your hands up, but when you're defending, stay low." This changed how I played completely.

After that first game in Arizona, Berger was so pissed that he wanted to leave in a separate vehicle.

"You just embarrassed us. I don't even wanna walk out with y'all. I'm going out the front. You guys are going out the back."

I said to Val, "Oh my god, Coach is so mad. What are we going to do? I've never seen a coach do that before." We were out of town; he was our only adult (even though we were in college); he was abandoning us; we were devastated.

It should have shaken us up for the second game, but it made no difference. We were just in our heads, far from home, in a different gymnasium . . . Who the fuck knows what was going on, but in the second game we were getting beaten yet again, this time by twenty-two points.

And Coach Berger didn't play that shit.

There's something about me you should know: I can hype the fuck outta shit, can get people so fired up just by being me. I can even feel that energy leave my body—it's like an aerosol or something that I shoot out. That day in Arizona I could feel it, even though I didn't fully understand it.

I went over to Coach Berger.

"Put me in," I said.

He just looked at me, and I think he saw something, too.

So, he did, he put me in, and on that court that night I went apeshit fucking crazy. I was snatching rebounds and scoring and just getting my team so hyped. At one point I grabbed a rebound, and you could hear the slap of the ball on my palms all across Arizona. "We got this shit!" I screamed. Me getting activated in turn activated Leone—she kept high-fiving me, feeding off my energy. The game went to the wire, but in the end, we beat Arizona by two points.

After the game, Berger was in tears.

"I've never seen anything like that before," he said. "I'm so proud of you. I just knew you guys could do it."

We went to a 7-Eleven afterwards for snacks. I wanted two donuts. Coach Berger said, "You can have whatever the fuck you want."

It was one of the highlights of my life, that game. I had felt an incredible power inside me—no one was going to fuck with me—and I had used that power to dominate a basketball game and bring us back from the dead. There would be many times in the coming years when I'd have to pull on that power in other ways, too.

I had not been getting along with my dad much before I left for Chapman. It was my fault . . . I hated him for what he had become and hated what the house had become—I was eighteen, and just hated life.

I can see now that my dad was probably depressed; he wanted to be successful, but it hadn't happened. He wasn't the man he wanted to be. When he sent me to college he gave me his last thirty dollars—a twenty and two fives. Men didn't show their emotions much then, but he cared so much about me.

If you're reading this now, and you're eighteen, or younger, get your ass up and go hug your parents and thank them. You don't have to mean it; just say it.

And if you're older than that, call them and say, "I get it, Ma. I get it, Daddy." It's a cold world without your parents, the two people who unconditionally love you.

———————

At the end of my first semester, my team had been on the road for a game in Utah. In Salt Lake City airport on the way back, I fell asleep and had a dream about my mother. She was in the middle of a silver table, in a white gown, just lying there in the fetal position. The whole room was white, except for the silver table . . . When I woke up, I felt so strange, and I think I knew something was wrong. I ran to find a pay phone and called home.

My brother was crying.

"What's going on?" I said.

"Something's wrong with Mom," he said. "They just took her to the hospital." The plane was ready to leave, and I had to run to make it. And that was all I knew until I got back to Chapman and called home again.

"I'm on my way," I told my dad.

"Don't," Dad said, "she's fine. She'll be in the hospital a couple of days, but she's going to be OK."

"What is it?" I asked. "What happened?"

"Oh, you know, she just had a spell," he said. "She's fine."

The next day, I got a call from my cousin.

"Why the fuck is you not down here?" she said.

"What are you talking about?" I said. "Daddy said that she was fine."

"She's not fine," my cousin said. "Your mom had a stroke."

If my mom had died, I would have never forgiven my father. He thought he was protecting me, but I needed to know. What the fuck would he have told me if she had died? I flew to that hospital, and when I walked in her sisters were in the waiting room, so I knew it was serious because we didn't really fuck with that side of the family.

I was taken in to see my mom. They'd shaven her head to make an incision to relieve the pressure from the stroke. Honestly, when I saw all the wires, it didn't look like her and I didn't believe that that was my mother.

"That's not my mother y'all," I said. "You have the wrong person. Take me to my mom!"

I couldn't communicate with her. She was supposed to die; this was different this time. I was so scared for my brother, too—he had been there when she had the stroke, and I knew it was going to fuck him up even more.

I sat with her, with all the wires in her, and I thought, *You'll never be the same after this. You're not you. You're not going to be my mother anymore. We've come to this point.*

I loved my mother, and I went and saw her as much as I could. But I do believe I said goodbye to her that day.

The memory that still keeps me up at night is the last time I saw my mother before she had her stroke. She didn't have any money, and borrowed ten dollars from my cousin, Vicky.

"I only have ten dollars," she said, "but I'm going to give you five. I'll put the other five in the tank."

We were in the kitchen. The light was so bright in the house back then. The TV was on; there was food in the fridge; there was so much life in that house, no death there then. I watched her as she started to wash her hair at the sink . . .

I think I threw out a "hey, Mom, see you later . . ." You've got to speak to your people and tell them you love them when you can. I can't even tell you what I did with that five dollars. I was just a stupid fucking kid.

You see, so many times before, my mom had almost died. With her platelet problems, she'd twice woken up in a puddle of her own blood. I used to go to the hospital to see her all the time. But then my mom went back to smoking cigarettes, and now here we were, her about to be bedridden for the rest of her days. And she wouldn't take her medicine. I was angry; I wish she'd made a promise to herself instead of to God.

My mom was just thirty-eight when she had her stroke; I was eighteen, Keith fifteen. We were expecting her to die; it was a really bad brain injury. Can you imagine that? She was the link between all of us—me, my brother, my father. I had always been close with my father, but my mom really kept the family together. I knew things would be different going forward, but what I didn't know then was that she would be bedridden for the rest of her life, and my dad would have to take care of us. My grandmother, his mother, Cordelia—Big Mama—came down to help for a while. But then she got sick, too, and she had to go home. It was a mess.

I wonder if everything would have been easier if my mother had passed on then. I'm sure she didn't want to stay bedridden for the rest of her life.

———————

That first Christmas at Chapman I decided I wasn't going to go home at all. "This Bitch" invited me to stay with her— terrible idea all around. She felt sorry for me for a second, I think; I don't think she expected me to say yes, to be honest. But I did, and what a surprise—she just made me feel so unwelcome, and I had to call my father to come pick me up.

In the car on the way home he turned to me and said, "Why didn't you want to come home?"

"Because I don't feel like fighting you," I said. "I don't feel like fighting you at all . . . And this is fucking sad." And the house had death in it. The light in the house was hazy, dirty, death-like; everybody was sad. Dad sad; brother sad;

Mom sick. And I didn't want to see my mother that way. Who the fuck wants to go home to that shit? And as we drove along, I cried. There was no music on that day. Just me and my dad, on our way home. I could feel him thinking, *Please don't hate me, baby . . .*

(I wish now that they could see that none of their efforts raising me were wasted. That their kid made it. She made it.)

———————

My dad was drinking more and more. In Memphis when he drank, he was a party drinker, but he could still get quiet and sip in a dark corner back then. But in California, I'd get more sermons when he was drunk; there was an anger to him.

It would get to the point eventually where he was drinking so much that he would eat and then he would throw up all his food. One time I had to clean up after him, and I was so mad at him because he scared the shit out of Keith. My brother was crying, and I'm there cleaning this shit up and trying to calm my brother down.

My dad said, "Don't worry, son. It's OK, son. I'm alright."

But I knew this shit was fucked up. So, when I was home, I would make breakfast for my dad and on purpose I would fix him the runniest eggs. I knew he liked them runny, but if he was having a hangover, you know, not so much. *You don't want to admit that you drank too much and have a hangover . . . but you know I know, right?,* I'd think.

I had been miserable there for a while. I came home from work one day and my dad had made hamburgers. I went into the kitchen and fixed me a plate; I didn't speak to him and went to my room. Five minutes later he busted in.

"What's wrong with you?" he shouted. "You're fucking always frowning. Next time you come into this house you better have a smile on your face . . ."

I didn't know what he was he was going to do, or how he was going to react, so I just jumped up and hugged him. Maybe I could make him hug me back? Eventually, he put his arms around me.

"I know I've been really hard on you," he whispered. "Go eat your food and then get some sleep." I don't know if he cried after that; I don't know if he knew he was allowed to.

It took until I was his age then to realize what my dad was going through. His wife just had a stroke and left him with these two kids. He had not been involved in the day-to-day as much as my mom had. My mom wasn't my friend; she was my mom. She loved me, and we had fun together, but she was my mother. She knew what I was going through because she paid more attention to that stuff—being tall, getting bullied, not fitting in—and she was more involved because she was more connected to the school stuff. She was so good with me, and I knew that I could sometimes take advantage of that. She was just happy if I was happy. I often feel guilty about how I treated her. I know how much she worried about me.

But my dad was only thirty-nine years old when my mom got so sick. Can you imagine what that man went through? How scared he was? He couldn't show it to us; maybe he cried when we weren't around—who knows? And it's not as if he had two little wallflowers for kids—no, he had two rebellious, crazy kids who were not kids anymore.

My brother became one of the biggest dope dealers on his block. He was even selling crack to one of my teachers. But it was so hard to avoid it in the eighties. Everyone knew he'd fucked up—my parents, the teachers (except the one buying from him), and sports coaches (Keith was a good football player). But none of us could save him. It wasn't that we were overly close, but I was his big sister, so he gave me the courtesy of hearing me out when I tried to talk about what he was getting into. I didn't get very far.

"Man, they all trying to jump me into the gang. And it's just so much money." He kept saying that last bit over and over: It's just so much money, it's just so much money.

"But you were supposed to be a football player," I said, but he was already there and in it and he wasn't going to listen to me or anyone. What people don't understand is that when you're in that bubble, you have to survive it. If you've ever seen movies like *New Jack City*, you know the crack era was a thing—it hit impoverished neighborhoods hard. Any young kid who didn't have a scholarship or job prospects or money . . . they ended up selling drugs. And yeah, there's a lot of kids who *didn't* do it, but my brother, he just got caught up in it. Unless you lived through it, you can never know what it was like.

———————

Even before my mom got sick, I had known that I had to get out of Lynwood. I didn't want to be like my friends who'd gotten pregnant and stuck there. But I knew that I had to get the fuck out of that house, so going to Chapman had been a lifesaver. Once Mom got sick, though, I really didn't like going back home at all because it felt like death; it even smelled like death.

And I had a boyfriend now.

I met Richard Brooks at a charity basketball game at Chapman. I'd seen him in the gym once or twice before, watching us practice. I just thought it was some guy from the neighborhood.

Up to that point, I hadn't had much luck with men—crushes here and there—but the charity event promised more luck. Some players from the Rams were going to play the alumni, and the alumni from Chapman are all Black, and they were as fine as a muthafucka, so me and Val went along to check it out.

Turned out Richard was there again—he was an alumnus. I noticed this time that he was fine—I thought he looked like James Worthy. After the game I was standing next to Eric Dickerson, trying to get his autograph, when Dickerson's brother offered to sign something for me.

"Do you play football?" I said. ·

"No," he said, "I'm Eric's brother."

"Then why the fuck would I want your autograph?" I said. "I don't want the *brother* of the star's autograph."

As me and Val were laughing, she said, "That dude's cool," referring to Richard. "Let's get *his* autograph." It wasn't like he was famous either, but it was a move, so I made it.

Sure enough, he gave me his "autograph," but he also wrote the last seven digits of his phone number on the piece of paper. When I tried to call it later it didn't work—I was sure it was a 310, LA number.

"This muthafucka gave me a fake number," I said to my roommate.

"It's local, bitch," my roommate said. "It's 714."

When I finally reached him, I said, "Man, I had the wrong area code. You know I'm from Compton . . ." He laughed, we hit it off, we went out, and I fucked him on the first date.

I was eighteen, he was twenty-seven, and so began an on-off relationship that lasted years—too many years.

Richard was from Kentucky. When I met him, he worked with the blind . . . not really, he was just installing blinds. He had everything that I wanted from a man at the time: handsome, tall, big dick, a job, older, smarter. (I just liked hot boys—still do. I should be pickier, but I'm not.) Richard was my first boyfriend, so of course I thought that I was in love. He would come and pick me up in his truck, a black Chevy Blazer—in 1987 they were so in.

I just remember one night telling my dad all about him.

"You gotta be careful—I know you want better," Dad said. "You gotta be so much smarter than everybody else."

"Dad," I said, "Richard is the bomb. He has a truck. He also has a fish tank, cable, a futon, and a VCR."

"You dumb-ass muthafucka," Dad said, "*you* have a VCR. So you already got what this muthafucka got and more. And why the fuck would he put a fish tank in a one-bedroom?"

But Richard understood my humor. He would laugh at anything I said. He was one of the first people who said, "You are fucking hilarious." He would laugh so hard at me, and I thought that was so great. Making someone laugh like that? The best feeling.

Back in 1987, I wasn't technically a virgin, but I *was* a virgin, if that made sense. I'd never made real love with a grown-ass man. Richard took whatever innocence I had left.

After I met him, I really started leaving childhood shit behind. I'd jump on a moped at night, ride over to his house, fuck the shit out of him, and then leave, or he'd pick me up in his truck and we'd fuck in it.

When I got with Richard, I immediately became the cool kid because he lived off campus, and he'd show up and drive me away to dinners.

Leslie Jones had started to do what the fuck she wanted. She had a boyfriend who was older and lived off campus. I'd think, *I'm a different person. Hey, bitch, have fun with your high school bullshit. I'm getting fucked in a Chevy Blazer.*

My dad was still being very strict on me, then—I would shout at him, "I'm eighteen, you can't tell me what the fuck to do!"

During the summertime when I was home, in the mornings, even though he'd sobered up, he still had the rage of the alcoholic. He was already losing control of his kids, he was drunk, and Mom was sick.

I don't even remember what it was I'd done, but one day he said, "You're acting like a kid."

And even though I was scared to talk back, I shouted, "Cuz you treat me like a kid!"

And with that, he came over and slapped me in the face with his bare hand. Today, the grown me understands that he didn't feel like he had control and disciplining us was the only way he could get control. You can have whatever opinions you want about him hitting me but imagine trying to steer that shit and trying to keep his kids alive in the hood in the height of the crack era. He just wanted us to survive.

My brother jumped up and was going to fight him.

"Why would you hit her like that? You can't be hitting a woman like that!" my brother screamed—I just grabbed Keith, and my brother's screaming turned to crying.

I looked at my dad, and I could tell that he knew I was done with him. My dad walked out of the house. I'm sure he felt shame. I went out to where Richard was waiting in his truck. My whole face was swollen.

I got into the truck, and I just started crying. Richard took one look at my face and was about ready to get out. I stopped him.

"My father will shoot you," I said. "Just stay in the truck."

This was true—one night, there had been a party outside our house, and one of the gangsters in the neighborhood was pissing in our yard. Crazy Willie Jones Jr had gone out with his gun and said, "I have six bullets in this muthafucka, so that's six of y'all going down before you can even *get* to me."

They got out of there immediately.

"I'm not taking you back there," Richard said. "You're not going back there."

And still, to this day, I blame myself for that whole situation. I don't think I made things easier for my dad back then.

When I got back to school, I started to hang out with a lot of white folks and learned a lot about white culture. I was just trying to get away from the old crowd; I wanted a new set of friends. It was college; it was time to try new things.

The thing you notice when you're around white people is they have a freedom about them that they don't even realize is freedom. A lot of people are not racist; they've just never been around Black people. I remember one of the first times I realized the extent of the privilege was in Laguna Beach at this girl's mom's house. We were totally left alone; the mom was nowhere to be seen. And nobody was going to say anything about me going in the refrigerator to get something to eat whenever I wanted? If I did this at home, man! I just remember pickles; I always had to ask my dad for a pickle. Me and my brother were athletes and wanted to eat everything; it got to the point where we had to ask to get something out of the fridge. "That food has to last. If I don't stop y'all you will eat everything!" my dad would yell.

White privilege is freedom on a different type of level. And it wasn't just about a full refrigerator, it was every part of life. For example, white people are so privileged that they can openly be the hoes that some secretly are, if you get me. They have a type of whorism, or whoretity, that is just absolutely magnificent. I remember I was at a party once and some white girl was jacking off a dude in a hot tub.

All I could do was shake my head at some of the shit I saw.

"What are you doing?" I said. "Are you jacking this dude off?"

She was literally jacking the dude off while I was asking her if she was jacking the dude off. She started laughing but kept on jacking.

"Ew! Also, people are around. You not scared? You not ashamed?" But they just went on jacking and being jacked; later, they all slept in the same bed with each other, a whole crowd of them, and they fucked each other's men, all kinds of shit.

Me? I was never really engaged in that stuff because it was just so unethical. Not to mention unsanitary. (Honestly? For years I didn't get into any kind of pool or hot tub after that. I always called it "booty water." To this day, if someone swims in my pool, they have to sign a waiver that they won't pee in it. If they pee in my pool, they're peeing in my life, and I won't have that.) Instead, I was, as ever, the witness. I guess that's why I have so much material to draw on for the comedy. I've always been a watcher of people, an observer. But trust, I did not watch them have sex. Ew!

———————

Basketball was still the main thing, though. I thought it was going to take me wherever I was going to go, which back then was "overseas . . . to play basketball." After Coach Berger left, we got this goofy-ass coach whose methods were completely different to Coach Berger. I hadn't ever really loved basketball, but by the end of my sophomore year, it had started to become a chore, especially when that idiot coach did stupid things like turn the lights off before a game so we could visualize it. What the fuck? We were all fast asleep, right before tip-off! It was infuriating. I would disrespect that coach as much as I could—he didn't know what the fuck he was talking about.

But I was also funny—people liked me and laughed at me. Maybe I could turn it into acting or something if basketball didn't work out?

At the end of the year, the new Coach told me I wasn't going to have my scholarship renewed.

I took it well.

"Well, you shouldn't renew it," I said, "because I don't respect you as a coach. You shouldn't be coaching here, muthafucka. Fuck you and your mama. Y'all can suck all the dicks."

I don't know if I actually said all that, but I certainly implied it.

Anyway, after that lost year, the athletic director had found out that the new coach didn't renew my scholarship and had called Coach Berger in Colorado. Fortunately, he wanted me to join him there.

"I don't want you to end up back in Lynwood pushing a broom," Coach Berger would always say. He was really looking out for me for my father. (And you knew when he was bothered or mad, just like my dad—my first year with Berger, I was coughing on a plane, and I couldn't stop; Berger just slowly turned to look at me with steel eyes, and magically my cough dried up.)

I was going to do whatever I could to stay in school, even though I was not a school person. Basketball had indeed become a means to an end. Coach Berger got me a new scholarship, so I was heading north, to Fort Collins, and this time I would playing Division 1.

———————

No one told me that Colorado was a mile up in the air, and that means you will die from no oxygen.

The first thing Berger told me was that I had to get in shape.

"You have been away from discipline for too long," he said, referring to my lost year at Chapman, "but this is Division 1. You have to have discipline. I'm going to have to beat you the fuck up."

Colorado State was a culture shock. It's a big university, 130 people in classes, where at Chapman there had been three hundred in the whole school. Not to mention Fort Collins, where there were no Black people in the town.

Richard drove me all the way there, and I was loyal to him, except one time, but that was a dare, so it doesn't count.

Something else I didn't know was that you have to sit out a whole year when you get redshirted—you still have to do the practices and everything, but you don't get to play, and I was miserable. Coach was trying to do everything to make me happy, but I was not.

For a start, the team was mostly white. Now, I'm from the hood. I'm straight ghetto. So, imagine me showing up to a bunch of girls who had never met a Black person in real life. Like Sharon, for example, one of my new teammates.

"I've seen them on TV," Sharon said, "but I've never seen one in, like, real life—like, I've never actually talked to a Black person." Sharon wasn't racist at all—it was just that she just lived in a town of five hundred people and none of them were Black, so she had no idea.

Coach Berger made those sweet white girls run thirty suicides—in Colorado? Can you imagine how hard that was? Those girls weren't ready. No one made it.

Except me—I made it on the first time.

Coach said, "I'm not surprised—you were mentally ready."

Sharon was a big girl, and she clocked out after ten suicides. My job was to make sure Sharon got those thirty suicides.

So, I ran them with her.

"Let's fucking go! Fucking run!" I screamed.

When she finally finished all thirty, she fell over and cried—but I made her get up.

"Don't bend over," I shouted. "Get up! You can't just do that. Get up, walk that shit off!"

She was so pumped that she made it through that shit. We all went and got drunk.

Coach Berger loved me because I was so ghetto. Before the season even started, the first time they had ever met me, I had showed up at practice in a headband, carrying a boombox.

"Who got next?" I said to no one in particular. "I got next, right? I'm Leslie. Give me that," and I snatched a basketball from some girl. Berger and I had planned it ahead of time—he wanted me to intimidate those white girls. "Show 'em that street ball," he said.

During practice, as we were scrimmaging, I would block a shot and then knock that bitch out of bounds.

"You can't do that!" they'd wail.

———

Now in Division 1, you have to keep a certain grade point average. Added to that we'd have four hours of practice, then lift weights for two hours, and then go to the library and study for three. That was my whole day. By the time I got home it was eight, nine o'clock, and then I'd be expected to do that again the next day and the next. It started becoming like a job. I was not enjoying myself, and I started to realize that basketball wasn't what I wanted after all. And what was the point anyway, given that I wasn't even on the team? I'd find myself coming back to my apartment and drinking. But again, I wish I could quantum leap back and smack the shit out of myself. I was just sad for no reason, to be honest. I didn't have any friends and was so lonely, yes, but there was no reason to be as sad as I was.

I drank a lot. At one time I thought I was going to be a drug enforcement agent (which is pretty funny if you think about it). But to do so, I had to take a substance abuse course—and I would turn up drunk.

One day, the teacher stopped me after class.

"You're doing well here," he said, "but you're drunk every time you show up, you know that, right? Why do you think it's OK to drink like that? Or did you think I wouldn't notice?"

I honestly didn't need the fucking lecture. Whatever—that teacher told my coach, who realized I needed to get some friends, and sent me off to the Black student union, which was literally just a room in a building in the middle of campus. I walked past the open door three or four times, like I was doing a bit, and then I just walked right in.

"So," I announced, "this is where the Black people hang out!" Everyone fell out laughing. And that was the beginning of the light, because I had found my place. I finally felt at home for the first time in this town. I finally felt like I wasn't being looked at like a Black person. I didn't have to watch what I said, or how I dressed. I could be myself. And I met a great friend that day—her name was Denita Abernathy.

I was still partying too hard, though. Denita and I would buy a big bottle of Everclear—which is worse than moonshine—and we would mix that with Welch's grape juice, call it a purple passion, and get totally fucked up on it. Then we'd go to Subway and get one footlong steak and cheese sandwich and split it—we couldn't afford one each.

It went downhill from there. I started partying so much that I'd show up at practice, but I didn't give a fuck anymore. I would sleep through study lab. I was doing so badly in my classes. My grade point average reached a low of 1.7, nowhere near high enough to keep the scholarship. Coach Berger was fighting for me, but then something else happened.

At the Black student union, Denita and I would hang out all the time. We would party together, play pranks on people (there was one in which we put newspaper on people's windshields and would pack snow on top of it, then laugh as we heard people trying to scrape their windows clear in the mornings). But the best thing Denita ever did was enter me in a competition, because that competition changed my life forever.

Chapter Four

THE STUTTERING UNCLE

Denita Abernethy and I were walking through the quad at Colorado State one night (after our usual trip to Hardee's) when we saw a sign.

"Funniest Person on Campus Competition" it read.

"You should enter!" Denita said.

"Girl, no," I said, and figured that was that. I was a basketball player—what would I be doing in a comedy competition?

We went our separate ways, but a while later Denita came back and found me in my apartment.

"I entered you," she said.

"What?" I said.

"I entered you in the Funniest Person on Campus Competition."

"Why the fuck would you do that, Denita?"

I was mad, but not really. It was amazing that she believed in me like that.

"You think I could do it?" I said.

"You are funny," Denita said. "You do not know how funny you are."

My dad had always let me listen to Richard Pryor albums, Millie Jackson albums, Bill Cosby albums, anything by Redd Foxx, and I had my own Eddie Murphy album. I listened to it so much so that I felt that I was already an Eddie Murphy master, a Richard Pryor master, a Whoopi Goldberg master—I knew all their stuff by heart. Their comedy was already imprinted on me. I had already been studying the greats most of my life—besides Pryor, Murphy, Whoopi, geniuses like Buster Keaton, John Ritter, Flip Wilson, etc. Buster Keaton was one of the most important people to me because of the incredible physical stuff he'd do. I'd watch him with my brother, and we'd look at each other and just say, "This is insane."

I was also a Carol Burnett head, too, and I loved Lucille Ball. What was so fascinating to me about Lucille Ball was that she was so pretty, but she didn't give a fuck. Her face would be screwed up and yet she would still be so funny, and I remember thinking, *This bitch doesn't care!* I learned from her that you can't just act happy; you have to change your emotions to get your face to show real joy—same with confusion, or anger, or fear, or any emotion she wanted to show. She was a champ at that shit. It was a hard trick to learn, but it was valuable as fuck when I learned it.

I'd never even been to a live comedy show, and yet something about how Denita was certain I was funny gave me the inspiration. So, I created a whole set and tried it out on my friends. I talked about Black and white churches; I talked about my stuttering uncle, who lied a lot; and I wrote a sex joke. I don't think I wrote it all down; I just remembered it.

I also wrote a joke called "Use Your Titties," about my grandmother. The joke goes, "My grandmother made me help her put her bra on one time—it was fucking traumatizing. There was titty everywhere. *Here's titty, there's titty, everywhere there's titty titty, Old Big Mama had some titties, e-i-e-i-areola.* My grandfather would always tell her to use her titties whenever she got in trouble. One time we went fishing and she fell out of the boat; she was flopping around like a fish and grandad shouted, 'Use your titties! Use them big-ass titties!'"

I thought I was Eddie Murphy.

My friends thought it was hilarious. I was lucky that I was surrounded by friends who lifted me up. First, of course, was Denita, believing in me so much that she'd put my name up for the competition. But there were others, too. One friend, who was actually on her way to work, made a detour to take me to the mall to get me an outfit, and even got someone to do my hair. Another friend, Deidre, loaned me her dope-ass black leather jacket. I was so lucky that I had people like that.

And yes, in the traditional comedy way, I was dressed all in black. The set I'd prepared was about seven to ten minutes long, which is kinda too much for a new jack—meaning, a new comic—but I had no idea.

———————

At the time, I never imagined I would become who I am now. I really thought I was Eddie Murphy that night, though.

The entire basketball team showed up, and a bunch of my other friends, but I was still nervous. And there was a lot at stake—the winner would get to open for a comedy tour that was coming to the college. This meant that a ton of other new jack comedians showed up for the competition to try to win, working comics who clearly figured they could intimidate the rest of us. One blond chick in particular really tried to fuck with our heads, telling us, "You think you know about comedy? You don't know shit," and then I watched as she just kept drinking as the night wore on (it turned out to be a long-ass night). By the time it was her turn to work, she was wasted. And it did not go well.

And then it was my turn.

I was terrified. But as soon as I touched the mic, I knew I would be doing this the rest of my life.

It felt like I had finally found home.

I just knew. Everything fell away. My whole life flashed past my eyes. I could see everything. The nerves disappeared. And I just worked.

Those seven or so minutes were the start of my life. I felt completely comfortable. And then it was done, and everybody was going crazy; Denita said afterwards that I looked like a professional comedian up there.

When I finished, the MC came back onstage while everyone was losing their minds and said, "Holy shit—do you know that was the first time she ever performed? You guys."

They judged that night by whoever got the most applause . . . and that was me. I won; I was the Funniest Person on Campus.

The next day, the college paper, *The Rocky Mountain Collegian*, interviewed me.

I said, "I'm going to be the next Eddie Murphy . . . I want to be a professional comedian someday, and I figured this was a good opportunity. I think a good comedian should be able to relate to the audience and talk about things in a natural way."

I had no idea what I was saying.

After I won that contest, Denita and I went to a dance that the Kappas were hosting. Denita was bragging to everyone that I'd just won the Funniest Person On Campus—one thing led to another, and suddenly I found myself up on a stage.

Bad idea.

It was only the second time I'd ever performed, but when you're starting out, you're never as skilled as you think you are, and I came in cocky. And this time I was in front of Black folks and Black folks don't play that shit. Their attitude was "So you going to make us laugh? You better be funny as Eddie Murphy." At the time, Eddie Murphy and Richard Pryor were everything, so if you weren't as funny as them, then you just weren't funny.

Honestly, there were probably much funnier people in the audience than me. And I was still so green. Even though I tried, it didn't take long for people to be yelling, "Get the fuck offstage. What the fuck are you doing?"

I came down and Denita said, "It's OK. That's your second time. We going to get it . . ."

I had bombed like a 747.

But it didn't matter. I didn't care—I knew I wanted to do this, and I knew I was going to get this. Plus, I had won the chance to open for that comedy show that was coming to town, so I kept at it, practicing, and working on my set.

I was more afraid to not try comedy than to try it. *This shit right here is calling me*, I thought.

———————

Pretty soon after that, Coach Berger called me in to the gym and said, "I can't do anything else. You're not even actively trying to do what you're supposed to be doing. So, I have to take away your scholarship. I have to give it to somebody else. We will pay for the rest of the semester, but after that, it's over."

"That's OK," I said, "I'm going to be a comedian. I won Funniest Person on Campus, and I get to open up a show, and I'm going to do it."

"What?" he said. "Have you told your father?"

"No, I'm *going* to tell him," I said. "But I guess I'm going to have to tell him now, because you're taking away my scholarship, and this is fucked up that you brought me all the way out here to Colorado and then you basically said 'Fuck it.'"

"You're going to end up back in Lynwood behind a fucking broom, Leslie," Berger said.

"If that's what I have to do, then that's what I'm going to do," I said. "But I'm going to be a comedian."

Eventually, the professional gig came around. It was a regular campus comedy show, but it would be opened by me, a student. I wish I could remember who the three professional comedians were; I wish I'd journaled that shit. Because for me to walk into the room, the way that I did? Once again, I was so cocky. I was walking around saying, "Oh! They got free food for us and everything. We about to tear this place apart!"

This was a college gig, and a student was going to open for them? These would be professional comedians coming to a tough gig and having to deal with my green, wet-behind-the-ears ass. If that happened to me now, I'd be saying, "WTF is going on? How much time y'all giving to this muthafucka?"

Whoever they were, I can still see the faces of those comics: It didn't take a mind reader to realize they were thinking, *What the fuck? You won a little contest on campus? This bitch is going to bomb.*

That was bad enough, but when I went out to perform, I realized two things: one, the place was packed, and two, in the front row, his arms crossed, stony-faced, sat Coach Berger.

Why the fuck is he here? (I realize now that if I'd gone back to him then and told him I was going to work, he would have given me my scholarship back. But it was too late; comedy was now my thing.)

Berger's eyes were deep-blue mad, not calm-blue beautiful. I felt like my dad was there.

Then I made another rookie error: My stupid ass changed the set. I did some of the stuff I'd done to win the competition, but this time I wasn't hitting any of it right. I actually wrote new jokes for this show, too, but I'd written jokes I wasn't ready to do. I even did a period joke, and to this day, I don't do period jokes. I don't even remember what it was, except that it wasn't good, and it was gross. I was doing jokes like making fun of myself, too—it just wasn't funny. I should have stuck with the original set I'd won the competition with.

Coach Berger? He did not laugh one time. But then, not many other people laughed either. Once again, I'd bombed. Coach Berger didn't need to say anything—I could tell he was thinking, *So, you going to be a comedian, huh?*

And yet I still walked off and thought, *I'm going to do comedy. All this means is I have to learn how to do it right.*

———————

It was bad enough that Coach Berger had this attitude. Now, I had to tell my father.

I was excited and relieved, to be honest. I had found out what I wanted to do. I didn't want to work out anymore; I didn't want to run anymore; I didn't want to sweat. I just didn't want to do that shit anymore. It was in me—it was decided—*I am going to be a comedian.* Maybe I could stay in Colorado, get a loan or financial aid or something to stay in school. But deep down I thought, *Why are you staying in school, Leslie?*

So, I called my father to tell him that I lost my scholarship.

"Hey, Dad," I said. "So, yeah, so, I fucked up. I lost the scholarship."

My dad said, "What are you talking about?"

"I lost the scholarship."

"That's crazy," he said, "I'll talk to Coach. We'll get it straightened out—"

I interrupted him.

"I'm not doing good in school anyway. You have to keep a certain grade point average and it's not happening."

"What the fuck are you talking about?" my dad said. "You're not going to get this kind of opportunity again. I'm going to call Coach. Like I said, we're going to get it straightened out."

"I don't want you to call him. I don't want you to straighten it out. I don't want to play basketball anymore. I don't wanna do this."

My dad sounded confused.

"Well, what the fuck are you going to do?" he said. "This is the opportunity. And you're throwing it away. You're not going to come back here and do nothing."

Then I told him.

"I wanna be a comedian," I said.

"What?"

"Yeah," I said, "I wanna be a comedian."

"You wanna be a what?"

"I wanna be a comedian—"

It was his turn to interrupt me.

"Who the fuck told you that you was funny, Leslie?" he said. "You've never been funny to me. Ever. I've known you my whole fucking life. You've never made me laugh, ever."

In his anger and horror, he called out to my mom, who was ill in bed.

"Diane! Get up! It's Leslie on the phone. She thinks she's funny?"

Then he turned his ire back to me.

"What are you going to do?" he said.

"I'm going to be the next Eddie Murphy," I said.

"WHAT?! Eddie Murphy not even Eddie Murphy," my dad said exploding. "Are you stupid? Obviously, you've lost your fucking mind. How are you going to take care of yourself? Because you not coming back here and living in my fucking house, talking about how you going to be a fucking comedian . . ."

"I'm going to go live with Richard," I said. We were still dating long-distance.

Click.

My dad hung up on me.

It hurt, but more than the hurt, it meant that I was free. So even if I was hurt, I wouldn't have ever gone back there.

This is the truth: I really believed in myself, so much. I can't entirely explain it, except to say that comedy just felt so right.

So, it was worth it. I thought, *You're going to see, man. You're going to fucking see me do it.*

When I'd gotten onstage, it had felt like I was home. It was like putting a circle into a circle; it fit perfectly. And nothing was going to feel right until that was what I was doing full-time.

So, it was a crazy decision, but an easy one.

I'd started out thinking I'd be a professional basketball player overseas, but now here I was at the Denver airport trying to make a flight back to LA. Denita took me to my flight; she'd made me a batch of cookies, too, but I was late for the plane, running through the terminal, dropping the cookies, picking them up again, hugging her, crying . . . I didn't think I'd ever see her again.

"Bitch, I believe in you," she said.

"We'll keep in touch," I said through my tears. We hugged one last time, and I ran to the gangway and onto that plane back to LA.

Back in LA, Richard picked me up at the airport. On the way home, he made one stipulation.

"You're so funny," he said. "You make me laugh all the time. You'll be a comedian for sure. But you gotta get a job. I'm not going to even ask for money for bills, but you can't just be sitting around doing nothing."

This was fine by me—I wanted a job anyway. I'd always been a hard worker, and I wanted to have money, so I went out and got waitressing jobs.

But it was time to really do the comedy.

The first thing on our list was the Comedy Store on Sunset Boulevard. I remember thinking, *If you're going to do this, you need to do some research.* I called down there and found out they had an open mic night. I don't think I'd ever even been on Sunset before.

In those days, you could either put your name on a list and hope you'd make it up to the stage, or you could wait outside, and the bouncer, Chuy Castro, would come out and just point at people. So, by seven p.m. a line would form, and Chuy would do his thing. My first night there, at around eight p.m. he came out and saw me—the only tall Black girl—and I think he thought, *Well, that's different,* and he picked me.

I wouldn't go up until one a.m., but that was fine by me—Richard and I went down to Mel's Drive-In just along Sunset and just sat there until it was time. Richard didn't care; he was really encouraging.

"You're going to do this," he said. "We're going to do comedy!"

Then, after waiting all those hours, wondering what it would be like, it was time to finally go up, it went like this: I was introduced by a woman who was actually a really good comic—she had the audience laughing, and brought me up really nicely. But don't forget, I'm Eddie Murphy, I'm Richard Pryor, right? So I'm doing what I think they would do. I bounced up onstage, and as the woman walked away from my introduction, I just said, "White bitch . . ."

Immediately I could see that the audience was thinking, *No, no you didn't . . . OK, bitch, now you better back this cockiness up.*

But I couldn't, and I didn't—not even close. I was so nervous that I was mixing up the punch lines to my jokes. It was awful.

I could tell straightaway this was a lesson. I knew I was doing badly; no one was laughing, except Richard, and he was only laughing because he knew I was fucking up.

Let me pause a minute to tell you something about the Original Room at the Comedy Store.

The Original Room is a shaping room, an entity in and of itself—it has an aura. It is a living, breathing mechanism, a real thing existing within its own membrane. It contains the spirits of comics who have passed on. So, the comics who rule that room, rule that room. And if you come in with any type of disrespect? The room does not play like that.

Now, everyone there that night knew I was a comic, but they also knew I was on some bullshit. And nobody laughed. You could hear Richard in the back trying to be supportive, but that was about it.

The girl who brought me up went back onstage when I ended my set and said, "Yeah, give it up for muthafucka . . . and muthafucka . . . and shiiit . . . and muthafucka and muthafucka . . . and muthafucka . . . and shiiiiit . . . and muthafucka . . ." a perfect impression of what I had just done. It was beautiful, when I look back, how in that one bit she erased me.

I threw up right there, right where I was sitting.

And she didn't miss a beat.

"Yeah!" she said, "you're throwing up them badass jokes."

And yet I just remember thinking, *I still want to do it.*

Once I'd cleaned myself up, some guy came up to me and Richard. He looked like a fat version of Andy Warhol, with the bob haircut and the big, thick turtleneck sweater and everything.

"I have a club down the street, darling," Fake Andy Warhol said, "and you should come. You and your man. Come have a couple of drinks and look at the acts there."

So, we went to this tiny piano bar where they had a little stage. (I wonder now if that guy was trying to fuck me and Richard.) At the time, I just thought the place was so cute. There was a dude up there actively being Richard Pryor, just imitating him, and he was so good. I'd never seen anybody completely imitate Richard Pryor onstage before, and it put me back on track.

Things moved quickly after that. My friend at the time set herself up as my manager and was able to get me a spot on a show at a club called the World. The headliner that night would be Jamie Foxx. This was before Jamie Foxx was Jamie Foxx—I'd never seen him before—but he was obviously going to be something, even back then.

The World was a nightclub—Magic Johnson had a stake in it. It was where everybody used to go to party, and at the time, they had a comedy night. Me and a bunch of my friends showed up, and yet again, onstage, I did just as badly as before. I was trying to do jokes that didn't match me—they were "jokes," but they weren't comedy. Comedy is talking about life, and telling stories. You have to be able to really connect to whatever it is your material is about. If just telling any old shit makes you look like an amateur, then that's exactly what I looked like—I looked like a fucking amateur.

I was doing so badly, the DJ started scratching during my set—*zigga-zigga-zigga-zigga-zigga-zigga*—"Stop lying!" he sneered. *Zigga-zigga-zigga-zigga-zigga-zigga*—"It's a lie."

My friends wanted to fight everyone in the audience.

"We're gonna fuck you up, DJ!" they screamed.

I didn't know Jamie Foxx had watched the whole thing. When he went up, he did a really cool thing—without needing to, he said, "Let me tell y'all something. It takes a lot of bravery to get up here and try to perform. She really gave it her all. She don't know what the fuck she doing, but at least y'all give it up for her for doing it, because none of you muthafuckas did!"

Once the applause for me had died down, Jamie started performing, and I was revitalized in what I wanted to do all over again. He was so good—it inspired me. He did a joke where he was a preacher singing (he said his dad was a preacher), and I found myself thinking yet again, *I wanna be this person! This is it!*

So, after the show I sent my friend over to speak to his friend, Speedy, to see if Jamie would come with me and my friends to Fatburger so I could pick his brains. I wanted to know all about comedy; I wanted to know how to be a comedian for real.

I got him in the corner of that burger joint and said, "Please, you gotta tell me how to be."

"How old are you?" he said.

"I'm nineteen."

"You don't know shit," Jamie said. "You haven't done enough in your life to write a joke. Your life might be interesting to you, but you haven't lived long enough to know how to tell someone about it."

Then he looked at me and made sure I heard him. (I think I was also trying to come on to him at the time; I figured if I gave him some pussy, he'd give me even more information.)

"Go live your life," he said. "Go fuck. Go get fucked. Go get hired, go get fired, go quit jobs. Go get your heart broken; go break some hearts. Go live your life and make some material. Because right now you have none. That's why you're talking about your stuttering uncle. You don't even *know* your stuttering uncle. But when you learn how to tell a joke—that stuff about your stuttering uncle? You are gonna make that some funny shit."

And I did hear him, right there in Fatburger that night. Actually, I heard him a little too well.

I took his advice. I was not ready to do comedy. I understood what he was saying. It wasn't heartbreaking for me, because I knew I had to get my life together. I had to get a job; I had to live my life first. I was determined to come back to it, but it wasn't time yet.

So, I quit. For six years.

Chapter Five

SIX YEARS

I don't believe in being a starving comic. I believe in paying your bills. So, I was always realistic, and I always had a job.

For six years I was living life, just like Jamie said I should.

Because I was going to take a break and to try to work out how to be a comic, I figured in the meantime I should go for the best job I could get—might as well. It didn't matter what kind of job; Jamie hadn't said what kind of job, just to get a job. I was so young, I didn't know what the best job was, so I tried everything.

One of the things I applied for was to work for Orange County. It had a lot going for it: they offered a 401(k), it's hard to fire you from a government job, and if you stayed long enough you could get in the credit union. And best of all, it's really hard to fuck up.

So, they hired me, but I found out it's actually *not* that hard to fuck up and I fucked up a lot, so they just passed me round like a joint.

I had so many jobs for Orange County. At one point I was a justice of the peace, and I married people—those who were too lazy to have a wedding, or couples who had been together for years and just needed the paperwork. One guy came in annoyed that the whole thing was going to make him late for work. It was rare to get a romantic young couple, and when they did show up, they usually already had a bunch of kids in tow. Even though it might sound romantic to be the person who marries people, it was mostly just boring. I made sure that they heard me when they signed the paperwork that they were married, though—I always made a point of saying the word *married* very clearly! They needed to understand that there was no way back.

It was so boring, though, and I was forever fucking up the vows. I didn't know that it was "lawful wedded," so I used to say, "awful wedded."

I remember the judge calling me in.

"You know you're saying, '*awful* wedded,' right?"

"That's wrong?" I said.

"Read the card! It's *lawful*."

That judge liked me, though. He didn't laugh out loud, but I knew he was laughing on the inside.

The only time it was fun is when somebody would ask for a special ceremony.

Other than that, it was the same thing every day. Eventually it was clear even to my bosses that I hated it, so they sent me to a different department.

This time I was a runner for the judges, going down into the basement to get cases to bring up to chambers. The only way I could bear that job was to turn it into a fantasy—I'd pretend it was *Law & Order* or something, and I'd walk up and down the basement corridor or climb the little step stools all the time talking to myself in a deep voiceover: "Leslie Jones was the only one who could find the files for the judge, the files that would finally put this guy in jail . . . We caught you, muthafucka . . ."

Problem was, it was mostly little stupid traffic shit.

"This guy ran a red light, and we must see his face!"

My manager heard me one day.

"You're a weirdo," she said.

"But I'm getting the job done!" I said and went back to the voiceover.

Eventually I got bored with that, too, so they put me in the annulment office, which was next door to the marriage license office. I was seeing people that I had married not long ago coming in to get annulments. *Well, that's fucked up*, I'd think, and annul their asses anyway.

I took so many days off (they still had to pay you, so why not?), and honestly my old boss didn't give a fuck, but then a new woman became my manager, and she called me into her office one day.

"So you have missed a lot of days," she said, calmly. "We're going to let you go."

"Let me go? What do you mean? You mean to another department? That's cool . . ."

"No," she said, "you're done. The jig is up."

"So, no to the credit union, huh?" I said.

After that I worked for a catering service. That one was kind of fun at first, even though I had to take a bus to Irvine every day, which took forever. I was a lunch lady at an industrial site, and I swear I made that adventurous, too, because there was so much shit I would have to cook. They were paying me $1,500 a month, which was a lot at the time. But Richard started to notice that I was forever losing jobs.

"How the fuck does that keep happening?" he said. First of all I never fit the nine-to-five gig. Or I kept coming up against racist assholes who would try to belittle me. And I could not be quiet about it.

Like my manager at the catering service, Tom.

On weekends the company would send me to Laguna Beach to work in a country club, which was fun because we could take free food home with us. But back at Irvine one night, this muthafucka Tom—who looked like Freddie Mercury with the buck teeth and everything—accused me of not cleaning the goddamn ice cream machine.

"That's because I cleaned it in the middle of the shift and turned it off," I said. "So it's fucking clean."

Tom was still pissed about it.

"Look, Tom," I said. "The only reason I have even the tiniest amount of respect for you is because you are my manager. If you weren't, I would whoop your ass. Ain't nobody scared of you, Tom."

"You're fired," he said.

Turns out you can't threaten your manager.

I don't regret any of it, though, because all of it was exactly what I saw it to be. Tom thought he could just throw his weight around and I'd take it, but you know what, fuck you, dude—this is a cafeteria job. You ain't exactly making it, either. This is not a grand job in the middle of a great career.

There was one thing Richard didn't have to worry about, though, and that was even if I lost jobs, I always got another one, or two. Eventually I ended up working at Spoons Grill and Bar in Orange County as a waitress . . . and as a bartender . . . and as a hostess . . . and as a cook. I was also working a nighttime shift, twelve a.m. to six, for the post office. I knew I wanted to get something that would fit in with me being able to do comedy, and waitressing was always it. Beyond that, I was in my early twenties; I was roaming. I was also partying and becoming a Kappa sweetheart (I was only a Kappa sweetheart so I could fuck some of the frat). Basically I was crazy, a handful—but really, I was just being my age, living life like Jamie Foxx said I should.

Still I wasn't doing bits. I was not doing any comedy.

Things with Richard were getting harder and harder. Women fall in love with men who are like their father—that's usually the first man we love . So when I left my house, Richard literally was my father. (They even had the same birthday.) I went through a lot, living with Richard. He had respect for me, but I think he knew that I was too young for him, and I had started living my life. There was a nine-year age difference, which is a lot in your twenties, and I was never supposed to be in anything that heavy so early. Truth is, I lived with him because that was the only place I had.

But if I didn't leave that situation, I knew I was going to be stuck there. He was eventually going to get me pregnant again and this time he's not going to agree to me having an abortion—and that was not going to be good for me.

I knew I wasn't going to have children as far back as when I was twelve. I am not a pain person. You're telling me you're going to pull a whole human out of my pussy? (For a start, I'm going to need more than six weeks off.) We saw a film in health class called something like *The Beauty of Childbirth*—but all I saw was hideous shit. What's beautiful about snatching a baby out of a woman's ass? The fuck? My cousin Rhonda even delivered a baby in our house, and I remember that there was so much blood . . .

None of this was going to happen to me.

I was also so selfish; I didn't want to do that to my body, and I didn't want to be nobody's mama.

But I wasn't smart enough or taught how to use birth control. My mom got sick early in my life, and she wasn't there to teach me about it. So, the first time I got pregnant I was still living at home with my dad. I was eighteen. I was petrified my dad would find out, and my mother was bedridden, so apart from my one of my cousins, I had no one close to me who could help me.

All I felt was an urgency to not be pregnant. That was something that I never ever wanted to be. I never wanted to be a mother—I stub my toe and I have a problem, but you're asking me to carry a human around in my body like a backpack and then proceed to push it out the smallest hole in my body? And then raise it? I just felt that I was in trouble, and it had to be fixed.

But I had to handle all that shit by myself. I really raised myself in those important years. It's exactly what you want your parents to do—if my mom had been able, she would have yelled at me, but she also would have helped me work out what to do. But she was too sick, and I had to face the whole thing basically alone.

So, I had an abortion, and it was very hard. I don't want to say it was wrong, because to this day I would do the same thing. It's part of the young lives that we were living—hanging out with other girls you realize everyone is having sex and getting pregnant and it's all just part of life. But with the abortion, just the idea of having to go do this grown-ass thing, and I don't have my mom to help me?

I didn't have anyone.

This is what I tell everybody: Prevention is what we should be teaching. If I'd even had an inkling of how to protect myself . . . I didn't know any of that stuff. By my mid-twenties, I had had three abortions, and I thought, *This is not a birth control method.* As for Richard, he respected my choices, but in the realness of it, I don't think he was thrilled about my decision. And it wasn't as if he was committed to using protection either.

Planned Parenthood saved my life. I still give money to them to this day. When I went to Planned Parenthood, I finally learned how to prevent pregnancies and take care of myself. Thank God for those people and what they do.

It would've been so different if my mom was healthy. Looking back, I realize it was a mixture of grief and a little bit of anger that I had to do this on my own. I was already mad that my family had gone awry, with my dad's issues and my brother, and now I didn't have a mom to turn to, either.

As for Richard, eventually he and I became more like roommates. Our relationship became weird: father, daughter, girlfriend . . .

But things really went south when his mother came to stay.

———————

I was thinking about leaving Richard anyway, but we were at least doing OK by the time of her visit. Unfortunately, his mom never had any respect for me. She always thought I was a whore. Lord knows where she got that idea . . . the only person she spoke to about it was Richard.

But still, I was determined to fix up our apartment to impress her. So, I took all my checks—by then I was working two other jobs, and I even got a credit card from Macy's—and I bought all this shit for the house. I painted; I got new table-cloths and curtains; I fixed up the bathroom; got new linen and towels; I even cleaned out the car. I made the landlord,

Homer Simpson (his name was actually Homer Simpson, which was good, because he looked just like him), pull the carpet up so we could bomb the place three times to get rid of the roaches. I found blinds in the garage (Richard sold them, don't forget) and put them up. I built shelves.

I was a very efficient-ass bitch.

It was like a hotel by the time Richard got back from Kentucky where he was picking his mom up. He was impressed. But his mother? This bitch was the worst bitch. She didn't actually call me a prostitute, but when I made a meal one day, she refused to eat it, and I heard her say, "I don't know where she's been."

I tried to brush it off, but I just remember saying to Richard that night, "Are you not going to say anything?"

We were out in the garage at the time, hanging with Richard's really nice cousin.

The cousin said, "You know, Richard, Leslie's right—your mom's being kind of fucked up." Then she looked at me and said, "She's being kind of fucked up, and she knows she's being fucked up."

Richard's answer to all this was to fall back on the fact that he didn't want to say anything bad to his mother. Which was fine, except that when my father hit me in my face, he was all about fighting him. But now that it's his own mother?

I remember my mom always telling me: "You know when a dude has no respect for you." My dad would say the same thing.

So, I was done being nice to this bitch, and to her son, too.

One day during her visit she wanted to go to Venice Beach. I called my friend and told her to meet me there. Without Richard knowing, I packed my bags and slipped them into the back of his truck. I was wearing this cowl-neck, summer-fit, figure-hugging, hot city-girl dress—it was very Sade, who was huge at the time—and I remember his mother looking at me as if she was again thinking, *You're a whore.* (Richard's cousin, in contrast, said, "If I had a body like that, I'd wear that shit, too.")

That was the last straw—in my head I was thinking, *Fuck this bitch.* We eventually got to Venice Beach, and I hopped out, went to the back of the truck, got my bags, and started to walk away to my friend's car.

"Where you going?" Richard said.

"With my friend," I said. "You can fuck your mom, now. That's obviously what's going on here, because you ain't got no respect for me. You letting her talk to me any kind of way? We'll see how happy you are with her."

My friend and I drove away.

His mother did eventually apologize, but I was done with her, and Richard, mentally, by that point. Still, the back-and-forth with Richard went on forever—till 2010.

The worst part of all of that was that at one point I thought about how Richard's mother viewed me, and I found myself thinking, *Maybe she's right?* I was who I was. I was living the life that I was living. Maybe I wasn't the most perfect person for her son, but neither was her son for me, or for anyone. If she'd known all the dumb shit her son was doing—including giving me an STD and getting someone else pregnant—she wouldn't have judged me so harshly.

I lived in South LA for a while, riding the bus to Glendale, where I managed to work not once, but twice, for Scientologists. On those bus rides I was in another world—it took two hours each way—and I read novels, biographies, and history, and I thought a lot, and spent time inside my mind. You have to go through journeys in life, in-between times when you develop things like talent. Four hours a day I was on that bus making the most of it. It wasn't the hardest part of my life; it was just a time of my life. You get to be many things in life, even when you are in between. And I think that's what Jamie Foxx had been trying to tell me that night.

The first job in Glendale was doing surveys over the phone. It was about cars—I had to ask questions like, "Do you *like* your car? You bought the Ford *Whatever*, are you happy with it?" (To this day if I get caught on the phone by a survey, I always go through it because I know how hard it is to have to cold-call like that.) The Scientologists were forever promoting me at that job, but one of the ladies wanted to "hat" me, too, one day (meaning, move up the Scientology ladder).

"No, bitch, I'm a Christian. Fuck that hat shit."

Me and my friend eventually moved to Glendale, way closer to the job. But one day I was doing a survey, and the guy was trying to rush me off the phone. We got to one question that seemed like the same question repeated, so I skipped it. The lady heard me and fired me. This was a problem because they were paying me $400 a week, enough for rent and then some.

I went to work for a Scientologist construction company, setting up their appointments. That family was weird, though. The Scientologists kind of owned Glendale, and I started to get freaked out that one day I'd come to work and they'd lock me in there and never let me out or something.

The main guy in the family, in particular, acted like he owned me. I think they liked me, and I got the job done—but I do think he thought he was going to make me a Scientologist. And given that they had their tentacles in so much of Glendale, he found out I was interviewing somewhere else.

"I heard about your interview," he said one day.

"What do you mean you heard about my interview?"

"Your interview with another company. I know all about it."

"Well," I said, "they're paying more money and it's better hours."

"Yeah, OK, well, you're fired and you're not going to get that job over there either."

"I'm not fucking with you cult-ass muthafuckas," I said. "You can all suck a Scientologist dick. I'd rather join the Armenian gangsters on my street before fucking with you guys."

And that was the end of me and the Scientologists.

———

Next job was at UPS, but I had a month to kill before it started. Me and the friend I was living with were getting into unnecessary arguments because I had nothing going on.

You've got to have your own shit; you have to have a purpose, something to do. This is with anybody, anytime—any relationship, friendship, love, family, whatever—there has to be a purpose. When you've got too much time on your hands you end up obsessing on little bullshit. So instead of just hanging around doing nothing, I went down the street to a YWCA, where they were looking for basketball coaches for the kids' co-ed summer league.

I was a Black *woman* trying to become a coach, so the men gave me all of their leftovers to work with. So to add to the racial prejudice I always faced, I now came up against blatant sexism, too.

But what they didn't know, was that I'm Leslie Muthafuckin' Jones. I was intrigued—I knew that I knew about basketball. I was going to be good at it whatever *it* was I was doing. Just like my dad said. Be undeniable.

The kids were around ten to twelve years old, and I loved working with them. If I hadn't been a comedian, I might have been a coach. Part of the reason I love coaching is that I like to work off of people's best assets, off of their egos. Maybe it was something I learned early to protect myself— who knows? But these kids, these "leftovers," were so-called rejects for a reason. Other coaches had tried and failed, but I believe there's something valuable about everyone. Someone just has to show them. So the first thing I did was to go through each kid and find out what their strengths were.

There was one kid who had a lot of trouble with his mama and thought that he could get attention by being bad. I taught him that he could actually get more attention by being good instead, so we worked on making his jump shot better. He'd always had a beautiful shot; it was just that he sometimes took it when he shouldn't because he knew people would notice. Once I taught him he could get just as much—and better—attention by utilizing his jump shot correctly, there was no stopping him.

Then there was our point guard, a hot-dog kind of kid whose father was a coach. None of the other coaches would deal with that kid because his dad came to all the practices—and that's never a good situation. For a start, coaches think they get to coach all the time, and they tend to be too hard on their own kids, too, while still indulging them and believing them to be the best player. It's a toxic combination—especially when combined with a ponytail, which of course the dad had—but I wasn't having it. During our first practice I turned to Coach Ponytail and said, "I got it from here—you can sit down. You're not coaching him; *I'm* coaching him, and if you have a problem with that, you can take him home right now."

Once Coach Ponytail saw me coaching, he shut right up—and even told his kid to pay attention to everything I was saying. One of the first things I had to fix was the idea that kid had that he'd never be taken out of a game, but I quickly taught him that that wasn't the case at all. I would continually sit his ass down and make him watch other kids play "his" minutes. I think it's crucial that young people learn how to deal with rejection—and I think they should learn it from their parents and teachers so that they can deal with it in the real world later on. Fuck team participation—you need to feel that your ass can get rejected. When we lost, my dad used to say, "You'll get 'em next time," and I hated that, but he was right—he was teaching me how to deal with loss and rejection, and how to move on.

We also had some big-ass twins on our team. I understood those boys so well because I, too, had been one of the biggest kids growing up, and it can make you seem like a bully. Actually, those twins *were* bullies, but they had great parents, too, so I knew I could marshal their "exuberance" and turn them around. What I realized quickly was that all they needed was a mission.

"Look around!" I said to them. "You're the biggest kids on the team. You go to school with your teammates. They're getting fucked with at school, so watch out for each other. On and off the court! Protect the team!"

A few days later, our reserve point guard, a little kid who suffered from asthma, took me to one side.

"I don't know what you said to the twins," he whispered, "but I can go to lunch now without being picked on."

There was also one girl on the team who was tall, like I had been, and shy, like I had never been. I knew I had to teach her how to defend herself. There's a difference between fighting and defending yourself, and I've learned both: if you can carry yourself properly and show the world that you won't be fucked with, you probably won't ever have to fight. But this girl was always hunched over which was making her a target; I would sit her up straight. But even on the court she tried to be less than she was.

I sat her down one day.

"Whenever you get the ball," I said, "I need to hear you slap it in both hands, as hard and as loud as you can. And keep your elbows up at all times." I borrowed that trick from Leone Patterson. "Protect the ball at all times. And that attitude should continue off the court, too—when you go to your locker, walk upright, and when you close the locker door, don't *close* it—*slam* that muthafucka and walk away without looking back."

Needless to say, her mom loved me.

When I found out that kid played the cello, I couldn't resist expanding the advice about self-confidence to her choice of musical instrument.

"You haven't hit anybody with your cello stick yet?" I said one day. "You could fuck somebody up with that cello stick. You should try it." (By the way, I don't think she ever hit anyone—for a start, those sticks are fucking expensive.)

There was one other thing I worked on with all those so-called rejects—conditioning. By the second half of the season, they were outrunning everyone.

We won the league.

But the inspiration didn't just go one way—those kids made me go after my dream, too. They said, "You're going to push us? What about you? You say you're a comedian. When we going to see you do it?"

Which is ironic, because a little while later, my friend and I got into that same argument.

"How you wanna be a comedian, but you ain't even doing it," my friend said. "You called a radio station once and told a joke and won a contest? That's it—that's all you've done? You ain't done shit."

There was always a nagging feeling that I should be doing it. *When are you going to go up onstage again?* I'd think. I could never keep jobs—good jobs, with health insurance, benefits, all that—because I knew they weren't what I was supposed to be doing. Comedy was it.

I'd been living life like Jamie had told me to. I'd won the contest in college, I'd done some terrible gigs right after, I even took some classes at community college and did a brief stint as DJ Frosty on their radio station, I'd told a joke on a different radio show and won some shit, and I'd also been to Irvine Improv to watch their shows. (I'd also been involved in a pinch of looting during the LA riots. I got three TVs, a box of cellphones, and all the toiletries you'd ever need—my hallway looked like a well-stocked Target. That's nothing to do with comedy, but it *is* funny.)

I knew what the fuck I wanted to do, but my friend was right—I wasn't doing it. I was just waiting for the right time, but also it was fear. *Do I have enough material? Do I have jokes, even? Am I crazy? Should I keep a regular job?* . . . Actually, I think it was all just fear.

So, I went upstairs right after my fight with my friend, called 411, and asked for the number for a Black comedy club called Comedy Act Theater.

I called the club, but I was nervous as hell.

Michael Williams answered the phone.

"Are you the owner or the manager or something?" I said.

"Yeah, I own the club."

"Wow, you answer the phone?" I said. That got my first laugh.

"Well," I said, "I wanna come and do comedy. If I want to be a comedian, what do I have to do?"

"You think you're funny?" Michael said.

"Dude, I think I'm funny. But I don't know. I want to be the best there is. I don't want to waste anyone's time. I want to be respectful. I'd like to come and find out."

"Well, do you have any jokes?"

"I think I do," I said. "I think I got like seven minutes' worth of material."

"Come tomorrow night," he said.

And then I hung up the phone and went downstairs.

I announced to my friend, "I'll be at the Comedy Act Theater tomorrow night."

I prepared a set. A lot of it was about dating, but it was still a good set.

Next day, I got into my car, and drove to the club. My spot would be at seven thirty p.m.

I got there at five p.m.

I was sitting in the parking lot, talking to myself.

"You are stupid. You a stupid fucking bitch. Why the fuck would you do this to yourself? You don't have no jokes. You're dumb. You're dumb. What the fuck?"

I lit a joint.

"This is what you want to do before you go up onstage? You dumb-ass bitch. Put the weed down!"

The truth was, I was more scared to *not* do comedy than to get up there and *do* it. I would love to quantum leap back just to tell myself, "This is where you're supposed to be. You're not going to have a happy life without doing this."

At about seven fifteen I went inside and immediately learned my first lesson of comedy. A couple of comedians were already there, and when they asked me what jokes I had, I told them my entire set.

I knew immediately that was the wrong thing for me to do—I could tell they were going to try to get in my head.

"Hey, that's not funny."

"I've heard that joke before."

"You shouldn't talk about that shit."

But I come from pimps and hoes and crackheads. You can't hustle a hustler. I figured they must think I'm good, because they just gave me a whole bunch of rules about what I *can't* do. I learned from every eighties movie it was always about the big guy trying to buy the little guy's shit.

I take up space in your head for a reason, I thought. *If I didn't mean shit, you wouldn't talk to me.*

Then, a tall woman named Sharon appeared—she was the person who actually ran the club, and that bitch did not play. She was taller than me, had a Jheri curl, and was serious as fuck. (She always had cramps!)

"Michael told me you were coming," she said. "I hope you're funny."

I thought, *I hope I'm funny too, because you look like you will fuck me up if I'm not.*

Then, it was seven thirty, and I went up and I did my set, and nobody booed. I was relieved; I hadn't got crickets.

Actually, I got some laughs.

When I came offstage, Michael Williams told me I was funny. Even Tall Sharon was impressed. In my head I thought, *Next time, I'll be funnier.*

"You have potential," she said. "Keep writing more jokes and come back."

I drove home so happy, screaming at myself.

"What the fuck, are you crazy? Haha! You did it! You're crazy!"

But that was the start of it.

And yet every time I would go up, I would be getting ready to be introduced and I would think, *What are you doing? You are about to go onstage. Are you stupid?*

And yet I kept at it. I just knew.

From then on, I was starting to get booked. I would go to Comedy Act Theater whenever I could, and I would hit Maverick's Flat nightclub and do whatever spot I could get. I was still very dumb and had not learned to be humble. One night, I was parked in Ladera Heights smoking weed with a friend before I performed at Maverick's, and that made me cocky at the wrong time. J. Anthony Brown put me up, and I forgot my whole set. I just stood there, with nothing; waited a bit in silence; said goodnight; and ran.

I was not good enough to smoke weed before I worked.

In those few moments I'd been onstage saying nothing, my friend in the crowd had been miming to me, "Do the running joke."

I really should have known that joke off by heart, because it was something that actually happened to me.

The running joke was the first joke I wrote that people really laughed at me. My first real joke. It was also the first joke when I remember thinking, *Oh, you know how to do this.* I wanted to do something no one else was doing, so the actual running that punctuates the gag seemed like a good idea, and it was how I told the story to friends anyway. But that physical stuff was something fresh.

The joke was written about the time I was in a car with a guy on a date. He'd bought me dinner and then he said, "So, I bought you dinner, where we gon fuck?"

"Just because you bought me dinner doesn't mean you get to fuck me," I said.

He started going off on me.

"No, I bought you dinner so we fucking tonight!"

"Well," I said, "lets stop at this McDonald's for a caramel sundae. No nuts, because you want to hit me with yours, obviously."

That's the setup for the joke. The rest of the joke has us pulling up to the window to order and me screaming, "He's trying to fuck me!"

Then, in the joke, I mime jumping out of the car and running—he chases me with his car through the parking lot, and I run and run, and then the joke becomes a running joke. In the joke I say I didn't think he was going to chase me, but when I turn around: headlights! And I start running faster, which ends with me jumping in the bushes, getting on a bus, and leaving.

That's the joke. I got nominations for that joke from the *BET Comedy Awards*, when they still had them—it always killed.

But it's time to tell the real story.

What actually happened is that we went to a hotel, and I fucked that guy. I didn't want to, but I did.

That hurts my heart to even write this. Now, when I think about it, I just get mad at myself. I sometimes say to myself, "You could have just said fuck you and gone home." But I didn't—I just went and fucked him.

And to this day, when I wonder if it was rape, I have to say no. I agreed to go back with him. I sure didn't want to fuck him, but I did.

My therapist says by writing that joke, I just made that experience "livable"—I made it so that I was able to deal with it. But I still wish I'd gotten out of the car. I wish the joke is what really happened.

Men need to understand the position they put women in. I didn't think I was in danger at all—it was just more like I was concerned he would think I wasn't cool.

And women? You don't have to do it, ever. You can get out of the car. Fuck being cool. Get out of the car.

———————

I wanted to be John Ritter so badly—I thought he was the funniest thing. And I'd always loved Buster Keaton, too, of course. I just love physical comedy—I think that the funniest way to make a person laugh is to show them how to laugh. That's why slipping on a banana peel is genius. It works every time—every slip on a banana peel will always work forever. I was doing a ton of physical comedy (I still am). And back then, I was one of the few women doing the physical stuff. One joke then was about how I love buffets and I would do the Electric Slide all the way along it.

In a few months I was working my way up the rosters. But I was broke, and eventually I had to move, first from Glendale to a tiny place in North Hollywood and finally in with my brother's girlfriend's mother—that woman was housing all of us. I was trying to do comedy and really believed it was going to hit. But I had no money.

And I would pray to God, "I don't want to do this unless I'm the best."

Before God could answer, my brother walked into the house and said one of the meanest things ever.

"You ain't no comedian," he said. "This is some bullshit. I don't know what the fuck you're thinking. But you need to get a real job. You're not funny. You're embarrassing our family."

And then he repeated what my dad had said.

"I've never seen you be funny, ever."

I just wanted to scream at him and say "I'm really funny. You need to support me." But I figured he only thought that because he'd never come see me perform.

I was getting booked. And just because I wasn't making money didn't mean that I wasn't funny.

It would take another few years for the world to agree. Like I say, because I didn't believe in being a starving comic, I had to keep find ways to pay my bills.

That's when I found Roscoe's, and God.

Chapter Six

TABLE 5

My brother's baby mama was working at Roscoe's in Pasadena on North Lake Avenue and got me a job there.

It changed everything. I had a job I was determined to keep, the money was good, and I loved working at Roscoe's.

Not everything was going well. I was being kicked out of the place I was staying at the time. It was the scariest time—I was basically about to be homeless, just driving around looking for an apartment, terrified. I didn't know what to do. One day, I drove by a house that had a "For Rent" sign in the window, so I knocked on the door.

After a while, a guy opened up.

"Can I see the place you have for rent?"

He took me back to see this little back house on his property.

"How much is it?" I said.

"Six hundred to rent, six hundred to move in."

And that's when I burst into tears.

"Sir, I swear I'm not crazy," I said, between sobs. "I swear to God I'm not crazy."

I had on my Roscoe's uniform and apron, and I know I probably smelled like fried chicken.

"I just got off of work and they're putting me out of my apartment," I sobbed. "I don't know what the fuck to do."

The guy just stared at me.

"I swear to God I have the money," I said. "I have the money. I promise, I'll give you all the money after I get my next check. I'm a waitress, I make good tips . . ."

This could have gone either way, but there was something about this guy.

"Please let me live here, please," I wailed.

The guy looked at me, waited a beat, then said, "Just go get your stuff and move in."

It turns out Pete—that was his name—was the nicest hippie fucker you can imagine. He was a painter, and so kind. Later he'd even let me use his truck, he was that nice.

The situation with Pete was never going to be long-term, though—I was in this little back house, and it wasn't ideal, even though he'd been so kind to me and it was perfect for that moment. All of this felt like growing pains, but I knew I had to keep moving forward, keep persevering.

I hatched a plan to take over my friend Kelly's apartment in Altadena, north of Pasadena at the foot of the mountains. It was literally my dream place, but then it appeared that God didn't want me to have that dream because Kelly changed her mind and didn't leave after all, so I moved up the street from her to wait her out.

It felt like so many things were happening back then. I felt like I was on the cusp of something big, a kind of birth or something. I knew for sure, though, that I wasn't happy with who I was. I didn't know what the fuck I was doing; I didn't know where the fuck I was going.

And I was angry.

I was angry at the world. My mom wasn't here; my friends weren't shit; my brother was really torturing me, too, because my dad was taking his money. This, in turn, made my brother mad at me because he claimed I wasn't helping.

This was a really bad time between me and my father. He had become a man drowning; he was at rock bottom. He'd already fucked my credit up for years, opening accounts using my name and personal details—and I wasn't going to risk it getting any worse.

Honestly I think karma had stepped in because I couldn't really shame my dad for what he was doing to me or my brother. I had also done that same scam to a lot of people—it was so easy then. We did shit like this: You know back in the day when you filled out applications to get those credit cards from department stores like JCPenney and Saks? Well, you might not know this, but when you dropped them in that little slot, all that slot did was lead to a box under the register—not difficult to find a closed register, stick your hand in, grab a bunch of them, put them in your purse, and use the details to open fake credit cards.

All the people I did that with went to jail. I'm glad I stopped in time before I did.

So, what my dad did just came back to me. He had opened one of everything. He even had a card for Radio Shack—who the fuck has a Radio Shack card?—as well as loans, and refinance loans, and everything in between. It's one of the reasons I was so angry at him.

It was just fuckery all around.

One Sunday I was at work at Roscoe's. Everybody had made good money that day, and I was counting my tips when my brother's baby mama decided that she needed to say something about the situation with my brother and my dad.

"You need to give that money to your brother to take care of your daddy," she said, in front of everybody. My father was by then staying in a hotel, living off my brother's money. My mother was in a facility, a care home right off of El Segundo Boulevard in Compton. My dad had put her there when he could no longer look after her at home. We were mad at him, but it's not like we were helping him much, either, so what was he supposed to do? (To this day, when I get off the 110 at the El Segundo exit I think of her there . . . and I always think of the lavender sweater vest I used to steal from her closet. I loved that thing; she'd get so mad that I'd take it without telling her. She eventually gave it to me with a letter. Be nice to your parents. You may never get to see them again like you knew them.)

Dad was probably in his late forties; he's now in a motel, living off a son who was selling drugs. It was truly rock bottom.

Looking back at the fight between me and my brother's girl, I realize my brother was probably taking the shit with my dad out on her, but at the time I didn't need her bringing this shit to work and letting everybody know about our family issues. Fronting me in front of everyone? We could have had a private conversation about it.

"You need to mind your fucking business," I said. "Oh—and stay the fuck outta my business."

"But that's why you ain't shit," she said. "Your brother is spending all this money—"

I cut her off.

"Look here, you fucking bitch," I said. "You ain't gonna be the first or last bitch that my brother fucks—"

That was it—she took a swing at me. But I was too quick—I ducked and grabbed her, and we ended up sort of grappling with each other outside the restaurant. I tangled my hand in her hair just so I could rip a couple of shreds out of it, but eventually we got pulled apart.

I realized, then, that I was being held back by one of the waitresses there. The customers from table 5 tried to calm me down when I went back inside. Table 5 came in every Sunday after church, and I loved them—I was always sweet to them because they were sweet to me. I realized, too, that I was still calling her every *ho* and *muthafucka* I could come up with (even though it was a Sunday). The folks from table 5 had never seen me talk or act like that.

"No, no, no, baby. No, calm down!" the kind woman from table 5 was saying to me, but I had lost it.

"No!" I screamed. "Fuck this ho—I'm going to beat this ho's ass." It was just like the time at the pizza place all those years ago; I couldn't really hear what everyone was saying.

"Oh my God, Leslie, no, no, no," the lovely church lady from table 5 said.

I think I was still mad at everyone because I knew they'd blame me. Sure enough, because I'm the loudest, and because I called her every *ho* and *muthafucka* I could come up with, I was the one who got the blame. Howard, the manager, liked me, and once the dust had settled a bit, he shuffled me off to his car.

As we drove away and I calmed down, Howard said, "Sorry, Leslie, but you're suspended. The owner said so."

Of course he did—the owner had always had a soft spot for my brother's baby mama.

"I'm suspended but that bitch isn't?" I shouted.

Howard was a sweet man.

"The fuck is wrong with you?" he said. "Why would you start a fight like that?"

"Well, Howard," I said, "what I'm trying to do right now is figure out why the fuck you not talking to her like this? She's the one who started the fight."

"Because I don't expect that shit from you," he said. "I expect it from her. Not you. You don't act like that. Why you acting like that?"

"What the fuck am I supposed to do?" I said. "She pushed me."

This was the same thing as always—everybody was treating me like I was the only one being angry.

Well, I *was* angry—no one was looking at *why* I was angry, though. At the time, I was in so much conflict with people because I was in conflict with myself. Everybody was against me at the time.

Eventually I made it back to my apartment in Altadena. I went straight upstairs. I was so angry. I tore that place up—a full fucking tantrum, just went crazy.

But I had forgotten that I had scheduled a Mary Kay makeover that day. As I sat there in the wreckage of my apartment, out of breath, somebody knocked on the door. I opened up the door, and there was the Mary Kay woman named Cheryl Waters (who would soon become my friend). I must have looked completely loco.

"Hey," she said, staring at me. "Um, we, um, scheduled a facial today? Mary Kay? It's a great day for Mary Kay!"

And I just started crying once again.

What happened next is why it's important we Black women should always look out for and be friends to each other. There is a certain pain we understand.

"I'm coming inside," Cheryl said. "Close this door—nobody's gonna see you cry like this. I got you."

After I'd calmed down a bit, I started to explain to her about my brother and my dad and my mom and the dream apartment I didn't get and table 5 and Howard being disappointed in me and on and on and on. She just listened to me, let the storm blow out, and then she said, "Baby, do you believe in God?"

"Yes, of course," I said, calming down even more. "Yes, I believe in God."

"Then you should go to church with me," Cheryl said. "Come on—go to church with me."

Now, I'm from the South; we're raised in the church. We go to Bible study. But honestly I didn't have a personal relationship with God. God was a distant guy in the sky. That was religious bullshit. I was about to find a real, personal relationship with the God who had always been there.

And at the time, that's what saved my life.

———————

I started to go to Victory Bible Baptist Church with Cheryl, every Tuesday night and Sunday. It was the best thing that ever happened to me. I walked into love, straight into love in that church. God was already with me, though—I was already his child. Even after the things that had happened to me, I had always been in touch with him, but I didn't have a relationship with him. For the longest time I thought of him as a person who was just up in the sky, judging people. I was under the assumption that I couldn't go talk to him or be in presence with him until I got my life right.

But that's not what it is at all. I had it completely backwards. What I didn't understand was that I wasn't going to get right until I was in the presence of him. And that's what happened when I started going to Victory Bible Baptist in Pasadena. It was as if I'd found a family—I walked into love, walked into a congregation that accepted me.

This was a church where I could wear pants, for God's sake—unlike some other churches, they didn't care about stuff like that. They just cared about nourishing you as a person. It was beautiful to be in the church of people who looked like me—pure joy. I went to Bible study every week, and it felt like every time the pastor talked, or any time I was in a lesson, it was as if the gibberish that I'd been hearing for so long in my life turned into completely plain talk. Everything came to me in full understanding. It was just a rush of love and wonderfulness.

This wasn't about religion—religion is *human* shit. This was truly about creating a personal relationship with God.

Quickly I realized that God and that congregation brought me a joy that I never thought I could ever have. I literally separated myself from everything that had been happening and concentrated on me. I had to figure how to get my mind right, face all of my shit, get fully balanced in who I was, who I am now, what happened to me as a child, and where I wanted to be. Then I could get to the business of liking me for real.

And the only way to like yourself and truly know yourself is, I believe, through something bigger than you. For me, it was God.

I believe God knows you as you, and loves everything about you, imperfections and all. He is not surprised at who you are. And if I can know this love for myself through God, I'd be fine—better than fine. That type of love is bigger than you.

You have to go into your body and literally switch that positive shit on. No one can do it but you. And that's what I did for myself. I got the help I needed.

Looking back, I understand that this was all just supposed to happen. I'd lost my day shifts because of the fight, so I was switched to the night shift. No one makes money at night, and everybody knew why: the restaurant just wasn't the same. It definitely wasn't kept up like the day shift. I needed to make it more like the day shift.

"Look at this restaurant," I said one night. "It's disgusting."

Roscoe's had decided that the night shift staff might as well be a bunch of degenerates—or what they thought were degenerates at least. But I knew better. There was the cashier, Sueanne—she may have been eccentric, but she was also the most fun person as well as a brilliant painter. One of the waitresses, Anna, had four kids and a husband who kept running off to Mexico on her—but she was cool as shit, too, and became one of my good friends. Then there was Geraldo, who started out as a busboy but would become a waiter, and Geraldo knew how to dance, let me tell you. He had to be nearly fifty years old and he would dance all the way to the ground then all the way up. These were the so-called degenerate people who Roscoe's didn't think could work the daytime?

I beg to differ. I knew better. So I asked the manager if I could close the restaurant for a couple of hours in the afternoon—we were never busy from three to five p.m. anyway—and we got to work cleaning it, top to bottom. We cleaned that place until it was sparkling.

I realized that given what was happening to me in church and the work I was doing on myself, I was happy. I was finding another side of myself. I was meeting new people and realizing, finally, that I was just a human being, and that was enough.

I had found my friend Jesus again, and though I would definitely lose him and find him again, I realized that he's more interested in people who know they are not perfect than people who think they are. I was always thinking that I was supposed to be this perfect person, but he was like, "I'm not building you for that—I'm building you to reach people. You can reach people I can't. You talk to people I can't talk to. You can tell them that loving themselves is the way to love God. Because when you do that you can love others." (I wouldn't start realizing the full truth of that until after *SNL*.)

Who did Jesus hang out with? The sinners, the hos, the tax collectors. So why did I think I had to be perfect before I could be in his presence properly? All the people I'd been in conflict with—and a little bit of myself, too—had been feeding me the idea that I was evil. I learned now, being around a different element, that I was not evil—it was a lie I was telling myself. It made all the difference.

It's amazing when you finally realize that God is not surprised at who you are. You think he's sitting there saying, "I didn't know Leslie was like this! Oh my gosh!" No, he always knew me.

The lovely lady from table 5 noticed, too. All this time I had been making my way and becoming a different person, and people could see it. I was happy. After we'd fixed up the restaurant, we started making better money on the night shift, too. Around that time a waitress, who worked the day shift on Sundays, quit, and they needed to move somebody back to

Sundays during the day. The management didn't want me to leave the night shift because we had it working so well, but everybody voted for me to come back on Sundays at least.

"I'm not coming back unless I can go to church first," I said. Roscoe's agreed—someone else would help open the place up and I'd show up at ten, after church. I would come in there so happy—I literally felt like a light; I felt like I killed any negative energy that came near me.

And I remember that first Sunday back I went straight over to table 5.

"I see it, girl," the lovely church lady who'd tried to talk me down from the fight said, referring to the change in me, the light I was emitting. "I see it."

Everything started to get better. I was performing all over Pasadena, too, and LA, making all kinds of new friends—and even things with my brother started to improve. I was pulling it together.

Then Kelly finally moved to Atlanta and I got her apartment, my dream place. It was paradise. I had the whole side of a house, a big-ass bedroom, big-ass bathroom, big-ass dressing area, washing machine, dryer, huge kitchen, garage . . . All for $475 a month. It was the bomb, and right around the corner from Roscoe's—I could literally walk to work (though I didn't—most of the time I drove because I was a lazy bitch).

But whatever—even the girls who used to antagonize me now wanted to be my friend. I had become a different person.

I was still doing comedy, and I was conquering Pasadena. I was hardcore doing comedy by that time, and I was really putting the work in, doing the mirror time, writing the jokes, doing many sets. People were starting to pay attention. "You're funny!" they'd say. But I was also bombing—a lot! At first bombing feels terrible because it's embarrassing having everyone in the room go silent because you aren't funny. But bombing is also one of the most important tools that can shape you as a comic. You learn exactly what not to do, or exactly what to do, to fix the joke. You either will cut out what isn't working, or ride with it because you believe it will get funnier. You have to appreciate it when it happens, stick around—don't run to your car and speed off in tears—and take the ass whooping from the audience and other comics. That's how you learn. Reynaldo Rey made me sit next to him one night, right by the door, so everyone could pass me and tell me how bad I was, or say "oh next time . . ." or "you were good, but . . ." Bombing will always happen—you will get better, but as long as you perform there will be times when you bomb. So use it.

By then I'd been doing comedy for five or six years, from '93 to '98. Around that time the comedian Joe Blount told me that he was going to do some spots in New York, and I thought, *I want to go to New York.*

Dave Chappelle had seen me perform, too. "You a funny bitch," he said, "you should go to New York." Martin Lawrence also said, "You a funny big bitch."

These important, experienced voices were convincing me.

Then I got booked at a college career convention, opening up for Method Man and Redman. They paid me $3,000. So now I had money to be able to afford the trip east. Joe Blount ended up not going, so it was just me.

So, I did it—amidst all this wonderfulness I set out for a trip to New York. For a while, I would have to say goodbye to table 5.

Chapter Seven

ANGELS ACROSS AMERICA

Everything was falling into place.

In New York, I would go from apprentice to professional. That city unleashed a beast in me—and even better, I got paid doing it.

I went to visit New York while it was the slow season at Roscoe's—late August—and ended up staying for a month.

I flew into Newark Airport, but I had no idea that Newark was in New Jersey, not New York. When I realized I'd fucked up so badly by landing one whole state away, right there at the baggage carousel I started crying.

One of the cab drivers, seeing me in tears, offered to help me, and kept quoting a price, but I was so upset I thought he was trying to rob me.

"Please leave me alone," I said, terrified. Some guy saw it all and came over.

"Are you OK?" he said.

"This man keeps trying to take me to New York," I said, "and I need him to leave me alone."

"Calm down," the guy said. "He's just trying to help. And that's a good price. Don't worry that you're in New Jersey—a lot of people fly here because it's cheaper, and New York is just over the river."

Then I realized, this guy helping me wasn't just any guy—it was Brian McKnight.

"Go ahead and take this cab," Brian said. "He's a nice person."

"Well," I said to Brian, because I had to—I'm a comedian—"do I ever cross your mind?" (When I get scared, I make people laugh—myself, too.)

"No," Brian said, and walked off. (I met Brian years later, and we laughed about it. He admitted that people ask him that *all* the time.)

I had booked a Days Inn in downtown New York, but the room didn't have its own bathroom—there was one down the hall—and the whole place was so gross. I needed the community of comics to help me out. I had a super nervous breakdown on the phone with Rob Stapleton, but he calmed me down and told me to go get something to eat.

At the deli across the street, the guy behind the counter could tell I'd been crying.

"I'm going to make you a sandwich," he said, so kindly. "Don't be scared. New York is not scary. I know people tell you it's scary. It's just dark. And it looks like Gotham, but it's not scary."

And then he handed me the best chicken cutlet sandwich I ever had.

And then the New York comedians stepped up—I couch surfed at Dean Edwards's and Mike Epps's and Rudy Rush's apartments.

The first time I got paid in New York was after doing two sets one night at Jamique's comedy club, uptown. The first set I did, I was OK; I think I was really nervous. I wasn't really doing my set-set—I was just doing what I thought was safe. I remember coming offstage and the host, Terry Hodges, saying, "You was alright."

Oh no, no one's ever said I was alright, *I thought. So, it's my job tonight to prove to you and all these muthafuckas that I'm one of the funniest bitches you will ever meet.*

And then I went out for the second set and I de*stroyed.*

"Why you ain't do that the first show?" Terry said.

"I don't know," I said.

"When you out here, you do your best set all the time," he said.

Crystal clear.

Jamique came over to me and I thought he wanted to shake my hand, but actually he was sliding me money. When I looked down, it was $150. I ran over to Dean Edwards.

"Dean," I said, "I think dude just gave me money by mistake. I ain't giving it back. Let's go!"

Dean looked at me like I was out of my mind.

"They pay you for your work out here, Leslie," Dean said.

That was the first time I realized I could have a job as a comic.

"We got two more sets, and you going to get paid for each one of those, too," he said.

"Something that I do for fun?" I said. "You mean they're going to pay me for something I love to do? That's just fuckin' *crazy*."

———————

Next night we started at Red Eye, Rob Stapleton's club. I got paid $75 for that gig. I was on cloud nine.

The other comics couldn't wait to take me to certain spots to see if I was going to get laughs. After I'd gone up, they'd say, "Well, that's one of the hardest clubs in New York."

"Why y'all not telling me before I go up?" I'd say.

"We didn't wanna fuck up your head."

They took me to one club where it is known that people get up and turn their chairs around on the comic while they're performing. Me? They threw money at me. I was destroying those clubs out there.

BBQ's in the Bronx is the scariest club you could ever do in New York—the stage is tiny and set in the middle of a sea of people, all around you. The mic comes down from the ceiling, like a boxing ring . . . and that's exactly how I treated the gig, like a boxing match. By the end of my set, I had one side—where the women were sitting—chanting "Eat more pussy!" and the other side—where the men were—chanting "Suck more dick!"

I had those muthafuckas so hyped.

When I came offstage, the host of BBQ's, Capone, hugged me and said, "I don't know who the fuck you are, but you can come and perform here any time you want."

Riding home with the other comedians that night, they went on and on about how amazed they were at what I'd done. I noticed that in New York, the male comedians weren't scared to say a woman was funny, compared to in LA, where it was a lot harder to get respect.

The month had ended, and it was time to head back west. Before I'd left LA, I had thought LA comics were the shit, but when I got back, I just wasn't feeling it. They had made me laugh in so many ways, but when I got to New York it was a different level of comedy. I almost felt bamboozled by LA comics because they had me thinking they were the best.

In LA, I'd been doing well, but those LA comics wouldn't always give me love. There were some nice comics, but a lot of them were chauvinist, insecure children. But in New York, the men weren't scared to tell me I was funny as fuck— as a matter of fact, they used it to their advantage. "Oh, I got the only funny female comic" was their attitude. And New York was a bigger pond—there was plenty of work for everyone, and enough money to get paid.

I had fit right in in New York. New York loved me, and I loved New York. So, LA, you dead to me right now; I had to move back east.

But first I needed cash.

I worked three months at Roscoe's, slinging #13s and #9s. Plate after plate, table after table, I just sucked it up, stacked up my money, then it was time to get back to New York. I sold everything in my house: my couch, my bed, everything, and kept only what I could get into the green Ford Taurus I rented from Budget.

Here's how that went:

Budget: You got a credit card?

Leslie: Nope. I only have a debit card.

Budget: It says Visa on it, right?

Leslie: Yup, right there . . .

Budget: How about a Ford Taurus?

Leslie: You'll rent me a car without a credit card?

Budget: As far as we know, you got a credit card . . . it says Visa, right? OK. Sign here. And here. And here. And here. Initial here. And here. And sign here. And here.

It just seemed like everything was falling into place for me to go. I couldn't wait to get out of LA, but on the last night I decided to go see Richard before leaving.

It was the last hurrah of everything, and not just with Richard.

My brother wasn't speaking to me because he felt like I was leaving him. My mom was bedridden, in that facility. My dad was doing his thing. We weren't speaking. I wasn't really fucking with him. My brother, who was still selling dope, had been helping my dad for a little while. He was trying to be a good son, to get in good, like I was (he never understood he'd never get in good with my dad like me—he just wasn't my dad's first kid, like I was, and there was nothing he or I could do about that). Instead of trying to beat me, he needed to find his own way.

And it was time for me to be me.

———————

I drove to see Richard. "Inseparable" was playing on the radio. I remember thinking how appropriate it was.

I got to Richard's late that final night. He'd bought these Tulsa ribs I like from a restaurant I liked; we fucked. I was young, y'all. Whatever. Next morning, he let me sleep in for a little while, then he presented me with one last gift: he'd gotten me a AAA map book. These were the days before Google Maps, so that was great—he had planned my whole trip, stops and all.

One thing I knew: I wasn't going to drive through Texas. You can thank *Thelma & Louise* for that.

Never drive through Texas.

I left Richard's house around noon and went to my favorite taco place in Orange: Taqueria Mexico, on Glassell and Katella, beside a 7-Eleven. Best tacos in Southern California; when that store opened and I discovered it, it's no exaggeration to say that it became literally the best thing that ever happened in my life. The meat was so fresh.

So, at the start of my adventure, I got me eight tacos, and with the door of the Taurus wide open, I fucked them tacos up. Then I headed east.

My entire plan, beyond avoiding Texas because of *Thelma & Louise*, was this: No smoking weed while I was driving during the day. I wanted to be clear, not just so I was safe, but because it was a kind of spiritual journey, too. I wanted to talk to God and have a solid plan. That meant I was going to save the weed for the hotel at night, because I knew I was going to need it.

I avoided Vegas and headed to St. George, Utah. St. George, Utah, might be a perfectly nice place, but it's not a Leslie Jones kinda place. It turned out to be one of the creepiest places I've ever stayed. For a start, there was no one on the strip, and it was only eight in the evening.

I stopped in at a diner and ordered a cheeseburger. I had a really great bag of chronic in my pocket, so I was starting to feel less afraid. Cheeseburger annihilated, I headed to my Quality Inn, but somehow, in the meantime, I'd lost the bag of weed. So back I went, out on to the empty street—I swear to God there was an actual fucking tumbleweed blowing by—but no one at the diner had seen the weed. Yes, I asked—it was the chronic after all.

I wonder if they'd already smoked it. They did seem kinda chill about it . . .

Back at the hotel, the long drive and the talk with God and the lost weed and the movie *The Rapture* all conspired to bring my terror levels to 11—I didn't think I was going to get hurt or anything, but I didn't know where I was, and this country town was scaring me. I was too scared to get high (I had other weed besides the chronic). Turns out, this wouldn't be the worst bad motel experience I ever had as a comic.

Years later, I found myself in Bumfuck, Nowhere, during a show I'd done some crowd work. It was standard stuff—at one point, I'd made fun of some guy's wife. An hour later, there had been a bang on my motel room door. When I opened it, there was the guy whose spouse I'd made fun of.

"You really hurt my wife's feelings," the guy said, "and I'm going to need you to apologize." I found out later that the country-ass promoter had told him which room I was in, if you can believe it.

"Aw, man," I said, "it's all just jokes. My bad—she's beautiful."

This seemed to calm him down a bit, but as soon as he left, I packed up and fled.

This wasn't as bad as the time me, Donnell Rawlings, and Dean Edwards were booked to do a gig in Alabama. That cheap-ass promoter flew us into Atlanta and then made us drive the rest of the way; Rawlins had a broken leg, so it was difficult enough, but as we arrived in Alabama the fucker canceled the gig anyway.

To cap it all, the promoter put us up in some crackhead hotel. There was no way I was going to get any sleep on those sheets, so I called Dean and told him to come to my room, and he said the same thing—his sheets were nasty, too, plus his room didn't even have a TV.

Then, Donnell called us.

"Guys," he said, "you gotta come to my room. *Now!*"

We knew Donnell couldn't really move very fast, what with his leg in a cast, so we ran down there—only to find a real-life, actual crackhead in his room.

"Donnell!" I said, "why you tell us to come down here when you have company?"

"I don't have company, Leslie," he shouted. "I was asleep. I woke up, and there she was."

The woman looked at the three of us and said, "I ain't take nuthin'."

That was all to come. In St. George that night, I really didn't want to be alone; no one knew I was there; anything could happen. But I wanted so badly to get to New York, I was willing to do whatever it took.

As I drove out of St. George the next day, I thought about what I wanted to do with my life. I knew even then that I was never going to fool the universe. You can try all the tricks you want; you're still going to pay the piper. What if I'm supposed to lose? Well, then I guess I'm going to lose. If I'm supposed to win, I'm going to win. Whatever my jour-ney's supposed to be is going to be my journey—same for everybody. Change is going to be, no matter what—that's the only thing that doesn't change. Life is a constant: You think you're not like everybody else? Real talk: You are a replica of seventeen other muthafuckas.

Without entirely understanding it, I stumbled on something else during that drive: I was just happy. I was traveling, this wide, crazy country stretched out before me, Stuckey's off the freeway with my favorite beef jerky, the kind I used to get with my dad.

I was wearing a driving outfit, too: a white romper with pink flowers on it. Tennis shoes. My hair was pretty, and under the back seat, just in case, a Raven that fires six. I'm not a fan of guns but I loved that gun—it was so delicate and little and silver, though it would kill a man to death if need be. My brother gave it to me before I left. He said, "If you're going to travel alone on the road, you going to need a gun." At rest stops, I'd put the Raven in my pocket in case I came across a serial killer. I wasn't worried about getting busted for the gun. For the weed, yes. But mostly, I was worried about serial killers.

One day, somewhere in Kansas, I watched the sky get darker and darker—in those flat states, in the summer, you can literally see the weather coming up behind you like God pulling a curtain across the sky. Seeing that in my rearview mirror was almost as scary as my night in St. George— scary, but beautiful. Ahead of me, a gorgeous sunny day; behind me, torrential rain. I didn't want to get caught in a tornado, so I was flying. When the rain finally caught up with me, that's when I saw the sheriff. Of course, I slowed down, which meant of course he turned on his lights and pulled me over.

Bitch, you going to go to jail in Kansas. That's some bullshit. I'd never been pulled over like this. The weed was concealed somewhere; I wasn't stupid enough to have it out. That's also why I didn't smoke as I drove, either. And I wasn't worried about the gun, because I figured that out here in Kansas you could have a gun in a car (I found out later I was right about that). But all he had to do was search the car, or just even breathe deeply. It wasn't like *The French Connection*, where the drugs are in the running panels and it takes the entire movie to find them.

I knew I was in Hicktown, though, when I noticed that the sheriff's shirt was a whole different uniform from the pants. *So, this guy's the sheriff*, I thought, *but he's also probably the mailman and a short-order cook and the mayor and the only plumber. He's one of them white, goofy-ass Barney Fifes like you see on TV—he probably gets paid one salary to do all those jobs.*

Oh, great. I'm fucked.

"Was I speeding, officer?" I said.

He said, "You were, you were speeding a little bit. But what made me stop you is you slowed down and your license plate is California. So, I wanted to see what this was all about."

"Well, I'm driving to New York from California."

He just looked at all my stuff and said, "That's all your stuff?"

"Yep."

"Well, you shouldn't be speeding like that."

"I'm sorry," I said. "I'm by myself and just trying to get to the next town before it gets dark."

"Oh, OK," he said. "Well, you need to slow down. And I just really wanted to find out what you were doing. So, you going to New York?"

"Yeah, I'm going to New York."

"For what?"

"I'm going to be a comedian," I said.

"OK, well, you need to slow down."

"I'm kind of scared to drive right now," I said.

"Usually when it's raining like that, just pull over and let it stop. And then keep going. This is going to be over in a minute."

And then right when he said it, it stopped.

"Oh, you magic?" I said.

"It's a trick," he said. "Enjoy and have a good drive."

"Is there somewhere close I can stop?" I said.

"The next stop has a hotel with a Pizza Hut inside it. You should stop there."

He was the first angel of my trip. It would take till New York to meet the next one.

———————

Sure enough, there was a Pizza Hut in the hotel, and I stacked that salad up high to go alongside my twelve-inch Spicy Lover's Double Pepperoni. I took the whole thing up

to my room, locked the door, and jammed a chair behind—
the fears had returned.

I don't know what was doing the damage, but something
was. I think it might have been the feeling that New York
was still a hope, rather than a sure thing, and LA now felt
like a place I used to live, with people I used to love. So here
I was, adrift in Kansas, serial killers behind every motel
door, just so scared. After I'd eaten and smoked a joint, to
take my mind off my terror, I turned on the TV, and there
was John Ritter in *Problem Child*. I had seen this movie a
million times, but here, in Kansas, I found myself laughing
and bawling at it. I loved John Ritter so much, and I was so
comforted by him in that movie. I just remember saying
softly, over and over, "No one's going to hurt me while John
Ritter's here," until I finally fell asleep. (After John died, I
met one of his sons, and I told him that story. He said,
"That's who my dad was.")

———————

I arrived in St. Louis on July 4. There, I picked up my friend
Alysha Owens. She'd agreed to help me drive the rest of the
way but was confused by why it had taken me so long to get
to Missouri from California.

"I wasn't about to drive during the nighttime," I said.

"Well," Alysha said, "we're going to be driving straight
through to New York." This sounded like a great plan until I
realized that her idea of fun was to blast opera as we drove.

"I'm not listening to this shit much longer," I said, somewhere in Ohio, "so get this shit out of your system. What the fuck is wrong with you?"

I had managed to not throw myself out of the car so far, but by Pittsburgh I was done with Verdi or whatever-the-fuck, so I insisted that we listen to Luther Vandross instead. All across New Jersey we bellowed, "A house is not a home / When there's no one there to hold you tight!" until we approached the George Washington Bridge and New York City. Seeing the skyscrapers hushed us up.

We didn't know which freeway to take straight into the city, and we were in traffic. There we were, barely moving, windows down, looking at the map, lost. Out of nowhere a weird, bright glare appeared on our paper map, like a beautiful, heavenly reflection of something—turns out it was the light bouncing off a silver car as it pulled up next to us. The girl behind the wheel was stunningly beautiful—she had pale skin with light freckles, and dark, dark, wavy hair.

"Hey, you guys wondering how to get into New York?" she said through her open window. "Just get off right here—it will take you straight into the city."

I looked at Alysha.

"How cool is that?" I said, but when we looked back, the silver car and the beautiful girl were gone.

Had we dreamed her? Was she from somewhere else? I looked at Alysha and said, "Oh, she must have gotten off up ahead; let's catch up to her to thank her."

We never found her. Me and Alysha chalked it up to her being an angel.

Either way, she'd helped us find New York—now all I had to do was find somewhere to live, and comedy gigs, and a way into a better, newer, happier, safer life.

Chapter Eight

NOTHING TO DECLARE

I headed straight to Flatbush in Brooklyn.

Driving in New York was terrifying, but I had to get out to Flatbush because a guy had seen me do a set on my earlier trip and had offered me a couch to surf on if I ever got back out there, and so here I was. I parked that first night—I couldn't believe I'd found a spot, so fucking dope—and took my stuff upstairs, only to find the next day that the rental car had been towed. Dean Edwards took me to the Navy Yard to get the car, I paid $150 to get it out, and took it back to Budget. That was my first morning in New York.

I started working as many clubs as I could; I'd get home at three and four in the morning. The dude with the couch seemed cool with me getting in late, but I do think he thought there might be something else in my visit for him other than him being generous—I swear one night I could smell him jacking off (I always wondered why his house smelled like baloney). I had to do something—I told him I was going to put a futon in one of his spare rooms so I could have some privacy. But since he knew I wasn't going to have sex with him, I guess he decided to use me as childcare. Whenever his ten-year-old son came over, I was expected to babysit him—he just left me with the kid without asking. I felt sorry for that cute kid—I'd feed him, hang out with him—but I'm not a fucking babysitter. Then, after I'd worked till three in the morning (that's my job—I'm a fucking comic), he called me at six a.m. and told me I had to get the kid ready for school and bring him to the train. What??? Yet again I wasn't asked, just told, like it was my job.

I told him no.

That night, he came home and laid into me.

"My friends all tell me that you're taking advantage of me," he said.

Whoa. I'd been in New York about a month, and already I was in deep shit.

"I'm paying you to stay here," I said. "If anything, you're taking advantage of me. Because for one, you thought you were going to fuck me and that didn't happen, and then you thought I was going to babysit your kid—"

"You gotta leave," he said.

Welcome to New York.

I had nowhere to go, and that muthafucka was talking shit the whole time I was packing. I'd had enough.

"Hey, asshole, listen," I said. "You're talking so much shit, dude, you really need to leave me alone. What you don't know is, I have a gun, and I'm going to shoot you at this point. You better just leave the fucking room. You're trying to make me shoot you. I don't want to shoot you. But I will shoot your ass."

This seemed to get his attention, and I was left to pack in peace.

Out on the street a New York cabbie helped me with my stuff (yes, you read that right), and I ended up at Dean Edwards's place. He was out of town, but the now late Todd Lynn, who was also staying at Dean's, told me to come join him. We had a gig that night in Rhode Island—I carried all my shit upstairs and then got dressed and me and Todd went to Rhode Island. I was having to be really strong to not break in front of anybody. But I still actually had a great show that night—I think I made $250 or something. But Todd Lynn could be very insecure and mean, and on the way home, he just started in on me. "You gotta learn how to stay at people's houses when you're staying at people's houses," he said. "I heard from a couple of comedians when you came to visit here first time that they had to ask you to leave. Rudy Rush said you outstayed your welcome; Mike Epps, too."

Later I would find out that Rudy and Mike had never said anything like that, but that night I was distraught because all my shit was at Dean's place, and Todd Lynn was there, and I didn't know what the fuck to do. I remember crawling into this little corner on the floor, with all my stuff, making a cocoon for myself, and crying really quietly into my hands because I didn't want that muthafucka to hear me. I didn't want him to hear me being weak, so I just cried, so hard into my hands, and I just was praying to God. "God, OK, I know I may have messed up by coming to New York so soon without a solid plan. But you gotta get me out of this. What am I going to do?"

God didn't wait long to help me.

My friend Alysha called me and told me to come over; she made me a peanut butter and jelly sandwich that reminded me of the Little Rascals when they'd make them with the thick-ass bread. I just cried into that sandwich.

"It's OK, girl," she said. "It's gonna work out."

That very night I was working at the Boston Comedy Club on 3rd Street in the Village. The Boston was a legendary spot—Adam Sandler's first ever performance was there, and it had been an important place for a host of other performers (it closed in 2005). What I knew was, I still do comedy, and as I thought that, standing there outside the club, something came up over me, and this is usually when good things happen. Sometimes I'm able to just settle into what's going on. I remember standing there on the street, next to a fire station, and I was thinking, *Well, shit, you wanted a testimony, bitch. This is definitely you making it in this muthafuckin' city. You just gotta be positive. You gonna go in there and make some money. It's gonna be OK.*

Just as I was thinking all this, something amazing happened. Have you ever been in a situation where everything in the background turns black and white and all you see is this color object in the foreground? That's exactly what happened to me. There, on 3rd Street, stood this incredibly striking woman. It was as if she was another angel. She had this big-ass afro, and a gap in her teeth, and she was smiling so brightly, just walking on her way.

"Sis!" I shouted. "Damn, you are beautiful. What the fuck?"

When she opened her mouth, this beautiful Jamaican accent came out.

"Oh my God, thank you," she said.

"I swear to God I'm not crazy or anything," I said. "You're just really pretty. And I just want to stop you and tell you that."

Her name was Patsi. We got to talking for a while, and I told her I was a comedian, that I'd just moved to New York and was looking for a place to stay. After a while we said our goodbyes, and I went into the club to do my spot. Before I could start, though, someone told me there was a person outside who needed to talk to me, and sure enough, there she was, handing me her number. We hugged, and I went to do my set.

I ripped that night, went outside again, smoked a joint, and headed for the train. Down in the West 4th Street station, who's standing there but Patsi, now with her brother, Issa.

"Sis," Issa said, "we was just about to get on the train. And something told me to wait a second. So I got off the train. Then you just walked down the stairs."

Then he told me about the one-bedroom space he had in his apartment share. It was mine if I wanted it, and if I was OK with sharing with a bunch of Rastas.

OK with Rastas? I would never not have weed.

The room was spacious, the apartment was really cool, and the whole thing was just $350. Nesta (Issa's son), even came with me to get my futon from the first place I stayed.

"You put a woman out on the fucking street? You piece of shit," Nesta said to that guy as he pushed the door open.

For the two years that I lived with those Rastas I was really healthy—I never ate meat in the house. I was working clubs, mostly local spots, with the occasional road gig thrown in—Chicago, Atlanta, Philadelphia, DC, Delaware. I still was establishing myself, learning to be a real comic, and as a female comic I was doing well, though I wasn't really making a lot of money yet.

I was broke, and though the Rastas were really kind about it, they needed my rent.

At the time there was a Def Jam contest, and I figured I'd enter—the prize was $500, and that would go a long way. The contest was held at Caroline's, and it was won by Rich Vos, a white comedian, and everybody was pissed—it being a Def Jam event—so Bob Sumner, the co-creator of Def Jam, and Tina Graham, a main booker in New York, decided to do another one a few days later at the Peppermint Lounge.

The Rastas were clear that they weren't going to put me out, but they needed their money.

"I'm going to go do a contest tonight," I said. "If I don't win, I'm going to get a job tomorrow. Fuck this shit."

"Blessings," Issa said.

———————

But I knew I couldn't just be funny—I had to work this craft. As a female comic I was supposed to be afraid. I had guys jump on the stage, even pull their dicks out.

But it was paying off, and I was thinking, *I can't believe this shit is actually working out. I mean, just like I played it in my head, it's actually happening. I must be really funny* . . .

By this point, people knew that I was funny—that's why I was able to work in some of these places. But I was still new to the scene and wasn't making a lot of money yet. And this night was all heavy hitters, and in my head, I was thinking, *There's no way I'm winning this.* There was J.B. Smoove, Tony Roberts, Dean Edwards, Todd Lynn, Kool Bubba Ice . . . Given that I knew I didn't have a shot, I turned back to my pure ghetto days. I was thinking about how I could rob one of these fools so I could pay my rent. Back in the day, I might have been known to have done a little thing that can best be described as "You can't do a lot with your pants down." So there I was in the Peppermint Lounge scoping out the shortest muthafucka that I could take, but I am also thinking, *This is New York—I could lose my life. There's a pretty good chance that I might get shot. Because, if he's short, he's gonna have a gun.*

All this is going on in my head while the show is running, and I wasn't paying attention. What I was missing was that J.B. Smoove goes up, bombs; Tony Roberts goes up, bombs—even his big dick song, which is honestly hilarious, doesn't work.

I'm still not paying attention. Talent, the host, comes over.

"Are you watching this?" he said.

"Nah," I said, "I'm trying to find somebody I can rob so I can get my fucking rent money."

He looked at me like I had two heads.

"Hey, Tupac," he said, "come here. The fuck? You're not a fucking gangster. You're a fucking comic. I'm just gonna put your ass up next."

"What are you talking about?" I said, still not catching on.

"Are you not paying attention to the show?" he said. "The crowd is almost entirely female. They are not fucking with the other comics. I'm putting you up next."

So I went up, and started with a joke about *The Price Is Right*. "If that muthafucka Bob Barker called my name," I said, "I'm a gonna pop-lock all the way down contestants' row. [Then I would mimic dancing.] Pop, pop, pop . . . And if I bid, and you bid a fucking dollar after me, I'm gonna beat yo ass, 'cause I'm the one who's getting up on that stage with Bob . . ." And then I said, "If I'm on *Wheel of Fortune*? No, Pat, I won't be buying any vowels. You not gonna make me spend $250 on a muthafuckin' *E*. I need my money . . ." (I did that exact bit with Pat Sajak years later; he thought it was hilarious, but by that point I was rich enough to buy *all* the vowels. And that's exactly what I did.)

I was ripping. The crowd was screaming—I'd woken them the fuck up. All those men had come up with their male sex jokes, but I had read the room, did a few dating jokes, did a few men jokes, ended with "my name is Leslie, peace!" and those bitches were throwing money at me. (Even the New Jersey Nets dudes, who'd been in the corner the whole time, were going nuts.) I genuinely didn't really fully comprehend what had happened until I walked offstage and Tony Roberts grabbed me, spun me around, and said, "You just won this muthafucka!" Sure enough, I did win that night; I got the cash and a black Def Jam jacket, and on the way home in the car with Rich Lewis and Todd Lynn and Dean Edwards you could just feel how pissed Todd was. But I didn't care—I made everyone go to the bodega and get a sub, chips, and soda on me—$3.50 each, right there, that's love, son.

When I got home, the Rastas were still awake. I walked to the end of the hall in my Def Jam jacket, knocked on their door, announced I'd won, and they all went crazy. I handed over the rent money, and we partied until the first light of the new day, and then some.

Hanging out with a community of creative people was great. We wanted to be famous, but even more, we wanted to be funny. We wanted to create a joke that was totally new.

These were the days before cellphones, so bookers and comics would have to call my house to tell me about gigs. Once I moved to New York for good, I would keep a calendar book, and all the months would be packed, especially in the fall and winter. Walking up to clubs, I'd be thinking,

Who got the weed? Who going up first? Will I do some crowd work? On the day of a gig, I'd wake up, eat, play video games with my homeboy (a fellow comedian) on a PlayStation—writing jokes while we were doing so—take a nap, get dressed, head out to start in Brooklyn, maybe make it to Queens, three sets that night . . .

I even managed to spend a night in jail while I lived in New York.

Weed back then was sold out of bodegas. On Valentine's Day 1999, I was washing my clothes in a laundromat and decided to run across Clausen Avenue in Brooklyn and get me a ten sack. I had on my red sweats—I was wash-day dressed—and was wearing a colorful kufi hat, like the one Eddie Murphy wore in *The Golden Child*, and a midnight-blue pullover fleece. No bra.

The dude in the bodega sold me the ten sack and knew me from my comedy.

"Be careful," he said, "they're running up on mutha-fuckas. Doing a sweep."

I put the weed in my sweatpants, backwards and down so no one could see it and it would feel like a crease if you patted me down.

As soon as I left, cops rolled up on me.

"Do I need to get a woman cop to pat you down?" he said.

"Nah, I have a ten sack on me." Honestly, I figured I'd get a summons and that would be that. It was just a ten sack.

But since a cop had recently been shot by a guy on a summons, there was no summons that day. Instead, they put me in the back of a police car.

First stop was Central Booking. All I was thinking was *Don't send me to Rikers . . .*

The Black officer who booked me recognized me from the comedy, too.

"What are you doing here?" she said.

"Are they sending me to Rikers?" I asked.

"Probably not for a ten sack."

When they walked me to a cell, we passed the men's cells, and it was just plain eerie; it was like they were in a trance, trying so hard to keep in their own space.

I was terrified I was going to get shanked.

I went to sit up against a wall, looking tough, but eventually the other women spoke to me—we all stayed up all night talking. Everybody had a story.

Next morning the public defender arrived, and she was amazed I was there for a ten sack. We made it to court.

"Wait a minute, you had ten dollars of weed on you?" the judge said.

"Yes, your honor," I said.

"Am I ever gonna see you again?" he said.

"Not unless you see me on TV."

"Give her a subway token so she can get home," he said, annoyed at what a waste this all was.

"That's very kind of you, sir," I said.

———————

Secretly I'd grown weary of New York. I was missing LA, so after a couple of years there, in 2000, I headed back home.

By this point, my father was sick. He was drinking a lot, and whatever other ailments he had, he didn't make them any better by hitting the bottle so much. I'm pretty sure by this point he had cirrhosis, and a bad heart for sure. I think my dad knew that he was coming to an end, or that everything was coming to an end. While I was still in New York, one day he went to the facility where my mom was living—she'd been in a facility since 1987—put her in a truck, and started driving them east, back to Memphis. But by Arizona he'd had a heart attack, and my mother had developed sepsis, so my aunt had to fly there to get them both. I didn't find out until after it happened—my dad made my aunt not tell me. He was just so stubborn.

I can see now that my dad wanted to die in Memphis; back then, nothing made sense. So they both moved there, and my mom started doing really well in a new home—she was with people she loved and was getting visitors. It's different in the South because you're taken care of in a different type of way. When I went to see her, her hair had grown, and she looked good. I was so happy for her.

While he was there, my dad and I had a great talk on the phone. We came to a kind of peace with each other.

I asked him why he'd been so hard on me.

"I *was* hard on you, Leslie," he said, "but look where you are now. I've never had to take care of you. I've never had to bail you out of jail like your brother. I've never had to save your life. You saved your own life. Everything that I wanted you to become, you became. But your brother, he was another thing. We got tired, Leslie—tired of raising him. I wish we didn't. But you? You are your own person. I love you."

He told me he'd seen me on *ComicView* on BET.

"Did you think I was funny?" I said.

This was the man who'd once said, "Who the fuck told you that you was funny, Leslie? You've never been funny to me."

Now, all these years later, he'd changed his mind.

"Yeah," he said, "you were really funny. I want to be your manager." My dad would have been a great manager.

I was so proud to be able to send him $300. I had no money back then, but I found it to send to him. He was so happy with that.

Oh how I wish I could have that time back. He would never get to be my manager.

———————

In late 2000, I was living back in LA and booked to do a series of gigs in Europe, in Amsterdam to be exact. I knew my dad wasn't doing too well, but I always figured he'd rally—he was my dad, after all, a kind of Superman, always. He would get us the hotel that looked like a castle, he'd raised me to be myself, and I truly believed he'd live a long time.

My phone rang. I couldn't believe what I was hearing. I always thought my mother would be the first. Next day I had to head to the airport to fly to Amsterdam—I needed the money from that gig to pay for the funeral—but the cab driver didn't seem to know the way to LAX and I got there late, too late for the flight, and I was sobbing, and I refused to pay the cab driver and he was yelling at me and the guy at the airline desk was kindly booking me on the following day's flight.

In Amsterdam, I did the first gig and bombed so badly I had to apologize to the club owner. I did not realize my dad's death was really affecting me. I was so off that night, as though I'd never been onstage before. When I came offstage the guy who'd booked me found me crying again.

"Your dad just died," he said. "The fact that you walked out on that stage is everything. It's brave. I'm still going to pay you, of course."

"I promise to God, none of the shows would be like that from now on," I said. "I will get my shit together." I was thousands of miles away, just trying to make enough cash to bury my father. I was just a sad little girl trying to make it through those days.

Thank God for British comedian John Fealey, who was also on that trip. John was so sweet and hilarious, and I swear this guy is the original Austin Powers. After that first gig, we were all being interviewed by some French reporter, but he was pointedly ignoring me. John said, "Leslie's on the show, too."

"Yeah," the French guy said, "she was very bad. She *bermed.*" I'd never heard the word *bombed* with a French accent before, and it was hilarious.

"Yeah, it was pretty bad," I said, instead of punching the muthafucka. "I think I'm just still getting over the fact that my father passed away two days ago. I think I'm fucked up."

"Well," the reporter said, "ze show must go on, eh?"

With that, John stood up.

"Get the fuck out, dude," he said. "She just told you that her father died."

It was all completely surreal, especially as the reporter's girlfriend was there, and she kept flirting with me behind her boyfriend's back. I guess they do everything differently in Europe! But John was my hero that night!

But the most beautiful things were happening around me on that tour, too. Amsterdam was gorgeous; it wasn't my first time there but it was the first time I got to actually travel through the country; it was something my dad would have been so happy to know I'd experienced. I was in small bars drinking with these Europeans, singing songs, and I'm with John, who's a killer onstage. He could talk about a plastic bag for fifteen minutes and have you howling. One night I was eating like crazy, and he called me a cow, and we ended up laughing so hard. Then he stopped and said, "Leslie, you're so much funnier than your jokes."

"I feel complimented and insulted at the same time, John!" I said.

"Well, that's what you're supposed to feel like," he said. "Why don't you talk about your life? Talk about you. What do you feel?"

"I'd be too scared to get up and talk about a plastic bag for fifteen minutes like you do, John," I said. "I don't think I could do that without being scared."

"That's what you're supposed to be," he said. "Scared. You're supposed to feel what you're doing."

He looked at me, searching in my eyes for something I think he knew was in there.

"I know the history of my country," he said. "I know where my parents are from. Lots of Americans don't know enough about where they come from. You're just privileged. You eat twenty-four hours a day—no one's stopping you from becoming a fat muthafucka. All that freedom, but you still aren't discovering who you are. You especially, Leslie, need to find out who you are as a performer."

From that point on, I took to heart what he'd said. I started to be so much more myself onstage. I was doing physical stuff, John Ritter–style shit, being myself, so much myself. Maybe my dad was with me on that trip, who knows? "This is what I raised you for, baby girl," I could hear him saying.

And it worked—I ripped tonsils out the back of muthafucka's heads on that tour. Have you ever seen a person's head explode? Well, it was happening on that tour. And best of all, I was ripping in their language—I'd already picked up how to say "are you sucking dick?" in Dutch for a start: *Ben je aan het zuigen.* By the end of that trip, I was strong as fuck.

The last gig we did was back at that place where that French reporter had seen us, and he was there again. And when I say ripped, I mean, I *ripped*! They let me headline that night. Afterwards, we were standing by the bar, and the French guy and his girlfriend appeared again.

"Please," he said, "can I get an interview?"

"Nah, I'm good," I said.

"Oh Leslie, please. I want to apologize from the deepest parts of my heart."

And all the while his girlfriend was sitting there, just out of his eyeline, staring and smiling at me like before.

"You like me or something?" I said to her.

The reporter looked at her; she looked at me; and I just walked away, thinking about how my dad would have loved that.

Back in Memphis I went to meet my grandmother to see what kind of coffin they'd picked for my father.

"Y'all gonna put my daddy in a pink muthafuckin' coffin?" I said when I saw what they'd chosen. I knew my dad would laugh at that, but it was just so hard. I didn't stay for the funeral—I still had gigs to do to pay for it all. I found out, too, that some muthafucka had told my mother that my dad had died before I could get there to tell her. I ripped that muthafucka from front to back. I realized I was screaming at this guy in Willie Jones Jr's voice.

I just was so upset. I went to see my mom, to make sure she was OK. She seemed like she was thriving, but ever since her platelets issues and a bad blood transfusion, she'd had hepatitis C.

Six months after my dad died, I was living with someone who wasn't a good friend—she was just so irresponsible. One day she just happened to mention that there had been messages left for me about my mom. But the messages hadn't gotten to me in time, and by the time I heard them, it was too late.

Now I was an orphan.

I had to bury my mom, but I had no money, so my Aunt Amelia paid for it. Listen people: Get life insurance. Don't leave your loved ones to deal with burying someone with no money. It's horrible!

I believe when you're dead, you're dead. When I'd gone to bury my dad, I'd also gone to visit my mom. She was thriving, her hair was done, straightened like she liked it, and that was how I wanted to remember my mother, not in some coffin. So why would I go to the funeral? You can mourn, but let the dead take care of themselves. I had closure with both of them being gone and once again I leaned on my faith to get me through. I was in a good place with it. (My paternal grandmother made me swear I'd attend hers, so I did, but honestly, it was so ghetto that it was hilarious, people singing who couldn't sing, so it was worth it.)

Later that year I headed north to Canada to do a radio show. I had a great time; it was around my birthday, and they took me out to celebrate. I was smoking weed the whole time and the night before I was to head back to the States, we partied hard—so hard they had to take me from the party to the hotel to get my stuff and then directly to the airport.

I was standing in line, waiting to check in, happy as a clam. I'd only gotten paid $500, but I'd had a great time. I was off in my own world, not paying attention, not noticing the security guy with his dog standing nearby. Suddenly, the dog runs over, all excited, jumping up on me.

I was so high and the dog was so fluffy and nice and I don't usually like dogs!

"Oh my God," I said to the security guy, "your dog really likes me!"

I'd always been scared of dogs, so this was cool.

"Dude, your dog really loves me!" I said again.

"Yeah, he does. Come with me," the security guy said.

Oh no. I'm going to jail in Canada. I know I'm going to jail. The first thing I'm thinking is deniability—deny, deny, deny. In New York I told the truth and it didn't work, so here I'm gonna deny deny deny.

"The only thing to do is just be honest," the security guy said. "Do you have anything to declare?"

"Why are you asking me this?" I said. "And no, I don't have anything to declare."

"You don't have anything to declare?"

"No, I don't have anything to declare."

"Ma'am," he said—it's never good when they call you
ma'am—"do you have *anything* that you would like to declare?"

"No!" I repeated for what felt like the tenth time, "I don't
have nothing to declare!"

"Listen," he said, "the drug dog came over to you and it
jumped on you. And that means that you have drugs on you.
So, would you like to declare something?"

Does this muthafucka think I'm an idiot? I thought. *Yes, I
have a half a blunt in my pocket, and no, I'm not gonna tell you
that . . .*

"So nothing to declare?" he said. With that, the security
guy brought the dog back over, and by this time, honestly? I
hated that muthafuckin' dog. Especially when the dog went
right to the blunt.

You little son of a bitch. Fuck this fluffy dog.

"Do you have anything to declare?" he said one more
time.

The security guy reached into my pocket, and pulled the
blunt out.

"So," I said, "I would like to declare *that . . .*"

"Too late," he said. "That's why I kept asking you. Only
thing you had to do was say yes, I would've declared it, told
you that you can't take this out of Canada, thrown it out,
and maybe given you a ticket. But now, since you said you
had nothing to declare, I have to call the police. Just because
you decided to lie today."

*So wait a minute—you're not mad about the blunt, you're
mad about me lying?* Sure enough the cops came, but pretty
much immediately you could tell that I wasn't really going to

get into any serious trouble. They searched my bags and found maybe half a gram. I remember the cop looking at the security guy as if to say, "You called me down here for *this shit?*"

"You lied," the security guy said.

"I'll never lie again," I said, "at least not in Canada."

By this point everyone was laughing.

The cop said, "You don't have any outstanding warrants, you're clearly not a criminal. But for stuff like this, the fine will be $5,000 and you have to leave the country."

"Well, dude," I said, "I was leaving anyway, but I do not have $5,000. I have $500 that I just made—that's all the money I have."

"OK, we'll take that," he said.

"Please don't take all of it, it's all the money I have!" I said. So, they took $400, proving they were making this shit up as they went along.

When I got back to LA I called my friend to tell her what happened.

"You pet the dog?" she said, howling with laughter. "Did you catch its name?" But even though she had done her best to cheer me up, I was still kinda upset about losing most of my money that I just went to bed and knocked the fuck out.

I woke up next morning to my friend banging on my door. I thought someone was in the house, that there was a fire or something, or that we were in danger.

It was the morning of Tuesday, September 11, 2001.

Chapter Nine

WAS JESUS A REPUBLICAN?

After my parents died, I finally got my own place, on Kittridge off of Lankershim in North Hollywood. It wasn't easy, but I did it. I would spend the next ten years of my life there. Those ten years were filled with highs and lows and downs and ups and everything in between.

I had become a regular at the Comedy Store on Sunset Boulevard in the early 2000s, but I wasn't getting regular spots. Earlier, around 2008, I had gotten into it with its former booker. I had noticed that he didn't tend to book Black people in the Original Room. I knew I was funny. I wanted spots in that room and I had to go for it.

"Put me up at ten thirty," I said to him one day. "If I'm not funny, don't put me up again."

He put me up. And guess what? After that, I was up all the time.

I was hustling hard until the Katt Williams tour in 2008. I made almost $350,000 on that tour—it was the first time I made real money and felt like my career was booming—but I couldn't tell you where a penny of that money went in the end.

Someone wrote me a bad check at the start of that tour, so I didn't trust anybody, and I made Live Nation pay me in cash. After the tour, before a gig I was doing one night at the Laugh Factory in Long Beach, another comic on the show, Greg Fitzsimmons, asked me how much I'd made, and I said I wasn't sure about the total.

"Well, what does your accountant say?" Greg asked.

"I don't have an accountant, so I'm not sure exactly," I said.

"So what does your bank account say?"

"I deposit a lot of cash."

"Wait, I'm confused," he said. "Live Nation is paying you in *cash*?"

"Yeah," I said.

"You carried all that cash around with you?" he said, like he couldn't believe what he was hearing.

"Yeah—I had bank bags from Wells Fargo. They had little locks on them and everything."

Greg just looked at me like I was crazy.

"You fucking hillbilly!" he said. "You know someone could cut off those locks, right? And you think Live Nation is going to write you a bad check? They don't give a fuck about your measly $1,500 a show—they pay the Rolling Stones . . ."

We laughed so hard at me that night; by the time I went up, I was still crying laughing, and so grateful he gave me that advice.

Out of the Katt tour I got a manager and my Showtime special, *Problem Child*—for which I didn't get paid, by the way. Not a cent. They told me it was just good for my career and that I should be grateful. That was twenty years of my material, for nothing. And I never found out where the money went; don't know to this day.

I was doing a bunch of little TV shows here and there and played live a lot. I felt like I was always about to make it, always almost meeting the right people, almost.

All along, I was having to deal with a bunch of bullshit with my brother. As much as he said he loved me, God, he could be a fucking asshole. He started dating one of my ex-roommate's friends, even though he knew I wasn't friends with my roommate anymore. He would bring his friends over and party upstairs with them, leaving me downstairs.

"The fact that you're partying with girls who I'm not fucking with shows what you feel about me," I said one day. "'Cause it's always just 'Leslie and her shit,' never about the way those women treat me."

For a while back then my checks would go to his baby mama's house, and I would have to catch the bus over there to get them. One day I found out he'd just cashed them . . . One was for $60, one was for $40 or some shit. I needed that money—I had $3 to my name, and two of them I had to spend to get the bus. I went to find him—by now he was living with one of those girls I wasn't fucking with—banged on the door, and my brother just came out and threatened to call the police on me.

It was heartbreaking; I remember being on that bus on the way home just bawling. He had some of his shit in my apartment back then, and I told his girlfriend at her job to come over and get his stuff.

"Get his shit and get the fuck out my life, muthafucka," I said. "I'm done. Me and him are done."

The first time I went to New York he felt like I'd left him, and he didn't speak to me for a while; he always thought comedy was bullshit. But I'd send him stuff, clothes and Timberlands, and he had a job for a while, an apartment, his girlfriend lived with him. Then, when I was back in LA for good, I'd see him (if I had a car). But it was always up and down. For a little while, I didn't talk to him; I was so done with his shit. Then we worked it out, and he moved in with me, but eventually I ended up having to call the police to get him removed because he wanted to fight me.

That day we had been coming back from a laundromat in my car, and I was trying to help him, but he was just not listening.

"You're not even trying to get your shit together," I said. "You could just tell even by the way you were folding your clothes that you don't give a fuck about anything." The argument turned violent, so there we were in the car fighting and driving. He'd already been beating on his baby's mama before, so to him it wasn't anything to hit a woman, even after he saw my father hit me.

"Oh no, muthafucka, you gonna put your fucking hands on me? You gonna get the fuck up out of my house or fight me, and you're not going to win."

After that he became homeless—we went back and forth with that shit for a while. I was trying to help him. Because I'd done the Katt Williams tour and made decent money, I gave him $3,000 one time so he could find himself a place. Two days later he called me, needing more money.

It was so hard watching him deteriorate, having to take food and clothes and money to him on the street. It was the worst time; I didn't know what the fuck to do. My parents were gone, my brother was on the streets, I was trying to make a living, but it was hard.

My grandmother said to me, "You're doing right. He's a grown-ass man. If you don't watch out, you're both gonna die—you're both gonna sink in that same boat."

Around that time, I would have gigs here and there that kept the rent paid, and I had gotten a role in the movie *National Security* with Martin Lawrence. I was building a resume that would get me certain parts in films; Ice Cube already knew who I was.

One day, I went to an audition for a movie called *Lottery Ticket*. Me and Jason Weaver were in the waiting room; we were both ghetto, and we looked at each other and peeped the ghetto in each other—right away we knew we were going to get this shit. We got the parts. It would be shot in Atlanta, and before I left town to make it, I went to pick up Keith to bring him to the apartment so he could take a shower—I was going to be away for a while, and I wanted to make sure he was OK before I left.

On the way home, though, he started getting upset that he'd lost a blunt in my car.

"What the fuck?" I said. "If I get caught by the police with a blunt in the car, you fucking muthafucka . . ."

Later, I called him to apologize for yelling at him.

"I wish that I could stay at your house," he said, "but I know I can't. I know I messed up."

I just didn't know what to do about him. It was all very hard.

―――――――――

The next text I got from Keith, I was in Atlanta on the movie. He told me that he was going to Santa Barbara, where there was a chance for him to get a job. I was so hopeful; this felt like something good for him. I felt I could relax a bit and enjoy making the movie, but it turned out he'd been scammed—there was no job.

A couple of days later I got a call from someone who knew him who said they'd found him in a park in Santa Barbara. He hadn't been conscious when they'd picked him up, but he was on the mend now in the hospital, I was told. You have to understand when I got this call, it was like many other calls I got in the past with him, and once again I'm doing something big, and he is just in trouble again. His daughter went to see him. He left a voicemail for me saying he was OK, and I promised I'd call him when I got back to LA. I thought I had time. I thought, "I will just take care of it when I get home." I think that was a Thursday. Everything was a blur at this point.

Two days later my phone rang again. It was the hospital.

"What do you mean?" I said. "I don't understand. He was fine."

"Did he take something? Did he take something?" the woman was saying.

"Huh, why you asking me? I don't know—you're the fucking doctor. You tell me—did he take something?"

My brother was thirty-eight; he died a month before his birthday. My mom had her stroke at thirty-eight, too, so for the longest time I figured that's when I'd go.

My brother's story is just all sadness—it truly doesn't even have any meaning to it. His passing didn't mark some meaningful day. It was just sad.

The worst thing I'll probably ever say is this: When he had been so sick in the hospital, I'd thought, *Please, just let this be over.* I just wanted this whole thing to end. And I cry to this day because I think, *Did I ask God to kill my brother?*

I planned his funeral from that hotel room in Atlanta. The staff at the Hotel Palomar had been so kind, sending up hot chocolate every night. After my parents had died, I'd vowed to never not be able to afford another funeral or handle outstanding bills, so I'd gotten a life insurance policy for my brother. The wonderful man at the funeral home in Inglewood told me to bury him would be nine grand, but three grand to cremate.

Sold.

Some people are just so great at their jobs. That undertaker was on the phone with me every day. He went and got my brother's body from Santa Barbara, got a suit for him. He arranged everything and all I could keep saying was

"God bless you, brother. God bless you." I was able to give him some money and promised him the rest from my next check. He simply said, "I got you."

Meanwhile, everyone on the *Lottery Ticket* movie was so kind—Ice Cube, Brandon Jackson, Jason, Loretta Devine, all of them. Jason was in my room every night, smoking with me, making me laugh. Ice Cube flew me out to the funeral first class. When I got to LA I went and got my nails done, and then my hair—I was doing everything to avoid having to actually go to the funeral home to identify my brother. I called my grandmother crying.

"I don't wanna do this by myself," I wailed. "I'm so scared to do this by myself. Why the fuck am I always by myself?"

"I'm with you, baby," she said. "I'll be on the phone with you."

I remember reaching that parking lot and thinking, *I am about to walk into a funeral home. What is it going to be like? Are there gonna be dead bodies everywhere? Is it going to smell bad?* All the things you think when your mind is overwhelmed with grief.

And then I walked through that door, and the place was packed with family and friends. All my Cali family was there. My grandmother had called her sister and she and all her children were there. My brother's friends were there; everybody was there. I was crying so hard.

"Thank you so much for being here," I kept saying.

My great-aunt just said, "Did you think we were just going to let you do this by yourself?"

Cordelia, my first cousin once removed (she's the daughter of my grandmother's sister) grabbed my hand.

"We're going to be together," she said. "We will do this together." I was so thankful for them. My brother's best friend was there, too—Jeff. It was so good to see him; we'd been friends for years; we all grew up together. They all held me as we went up to the casket. Part of me was thinking, *They're going to open this casket, and it's not going to be him.*

But it was Keith after all, and yet instead of freaking out, I saw such peace. It was an incredibly calming feeling, and I thought, *OK, this is not my responsibility anymore. This is it. This is him. He's OK. This is the end.*

It was a calm peace; his journey was over. I could let him go now.

When it came time to say something at the funeral, I looked out at the few friends my brother had, and I knew I had to say words that would matter.

"I miss my brother," I said, "and I love my brother, but my brother made a lot of mistakes, and you muthafuckas need to grow up. He's dead because of the fucked-up mistakes that he made. Look at the consequences of what you do, look at the choices you make. That's all I can say." I was just so angry at him for not fighting. He left me alone.

After the funeral, I got taken out for a bunch of margaritas, got a beautiful hug from my little godson—babies just know—and thank God for Aunt Pat and Aunt Ann, too. They have been my rocks ever since.

Then I flew back to Atlanta to finish that movie.

After I got back from making *Lottery Ticket*, I was in a spiral. I cried a lot, laid on the floor a lot.

A comic friend, Ian Edwards, called me to do a gig. I didn't feel like doing my hair that day; I'd slept on it weird, so I thought, *Fuck it.* I had it short on the side, and it was sticking up in the middle, like a mohawk. Brandon Jackson had already seen it like that on set one morning already. He'd said, "That shit looks rock and roll."

So I just went with it.

After my brother died, a new me showed up. It was impossible to go back to being the same person after something like that happens to you. When you get somebody dying in your life that you didn't expect to die, that shit will fuck you up. Things suddenly became urgent. I now had one goal—to make it. And I don't mean making it like you might think I mean it.

By 2011, I had become a regular at the Comedy Store on Sunset Boulevard. Its former booker said, "We want to put your name on the sign out front."

I was already on the wall inside, listed as "Leslie"— that's all I went as back then.

"What's your last name?" he said.

"I just go by Leslie," I said. "You know, like Whoopi or Madonna."

"Whoopi's last name is Goldberg," he said, "and Madonna? Bitch, please, you could never . . ."

"I'm just Leslie—"

"Not going to do it," he said. "What the fuck is your last name?"

"Jones," I said, "my name is Leslie Jones."

"That's a star's name!" he shouted. "And that's your name from now on."

I was determined to make it on Leslie Jones's terms as Leslie, not as some compromised muthafucka. I want to be me. Nobody else. I'm going to laugh like me. I'm going to cry like me. I'm going to joke like me. I'm going to fight like me. There couldn't be anybody like me, because I am me already.

I was now ready to embrace that shit. *Let's fucking go.* So now, when I arrived at gigs, I didn't have time to sit and talk. No—where the fuck is the mic? Where's my money? No, I don't want to drink—give me my fucking money. I took to wearing these two long cloaks, and people would say I looked like a superhero when I showed up. Then I would go up onstage and do real material and rip and get the fuck out.

Also after my brother died, I think I actively went into trying to hurt myself. I moved into some condos across the street from the Church on the Way (to hell)—the church that owns that huge cross off of the 101 freeway in Hollywood (trust me, if you ever drive by you can't miss it). If you ask me it was no Victory Bible, but it was close to my condo, and it was a church, so I figured, why not? This was right around the same time I started fucking some guy. I found him on adultfriendfinder.com, but trust that there are no people acting like adults on adultfriendfinder.com, just a bunch of insecure jerks, which is what I wanted. This guy eventually became my Four-Year Booty Call. But nothing was going right then—I was not eating well, I was doing speed with him, and so I would go to this white-ass church, not realizing how right wing it was. I would have them all pray for me and then leave there and go and fuck the guy or do drugs with him. Being with him was a form of self-hurt; instead of cutting myself or becoming an unmanageable person, I did this. I never understood it. One friend said this guy was going to fuck up my career, but I still stayed with him.

I really wasn't noticing things that were happening in the church because I was so wrapped up in trying to get over my brother's death and fucking with the guy. At the church, I would beg for prayers, and one day someone said to me, "You want us to pray about you and that guy *again*?"

When you are in that state of pain you are looking for anything to take it away. I think I was trying to get to God but honestly I wasn't listening to him either. I wanted to be better, but another part of me was just acting out. So I was barely paying attention when some pastor started to rail on transgender people. And during another right-wing sermon, some dude saw me looking sideways at it, and slid over to me after the service.

"Republicans work hard for our money," he said. "We don't feel like we should have to take care of anyone. They didn't work for our money, we did, so it's ours. We should be able to do what we want with our money."

Actually, that one I heard loud and clear. And we were in church when he said it!

Was Jesus a Republican? I thought.

I even attended a Christian singles night lecture kind of thing—I was single, it was free, it was church. Honestly, that night should be an episode of *American Horror Story*. The woman leading it was telling us how God had cured her herpes (I didn't like to mention that herpes just goes into remission), and then another woman behind me stood up to testify.

"I'm thirty-five," she said, "and I'm a virgin."

The woman with or without herpes looked confused.

"Hey, let me take that one," I said. The woman leading the group looked relieved I was willing to step up.

"You need to understand something about God," I said. "I know that everybody goes by the scripture, but God really goes by your heart. And he has a personal relationship with you. You should really be talking to him about everything, because God doesn't hate anyone."

"But he hates the sin," the poor woman said.

"What sin do you think you committed?" I said. (It was pretty clear to me that the reason she was a virgin at thirty-five was that she was struggling with her sexuality, and thought it was a sin.)

I think that's when I started to want to be the person who says, "There's nothing wrong with you." I really wanted to help her but I didn't know how to help myself. I knew this church was not the way.

Meanwhile, the relationship with that random guy deteriorated into me stalking him, us fucking even while I stalked him, and me becoming friends with his dogs by feeding them bacon. Whenever he wanted me to stop stalking him, he'd try to sic those dogs on me, but they'd look at him as if to say, "No! We love her—she's the bacon lady."

None of this stopped him fucking me, note. (Cuz the pussy was the bomb—crazy bitches' pussy is always the bomb!)

I was doing the Comedy Store a lot at the time, at least four times a week. I didn't think I was going to blow up, and my hopes were starting to get battered again because I wasn't able to pay my rent some months. *Maybe a bitch's gonna have to go back to working regular jobs*, I sometimes thought. But I knew that I was funny as fuck—surely there was no reason that I was getting this funny for nothing.

Then Chris Rock saw me perform and told Lorne Michaels about me. Growing up, we thought *SNL* was a kooky little show. Sometimes you'd catch Steve Martin or Chevy Chase or Gilda Radner, but we only really watched it when a Black person was on it. When *SNL* hired me, I stopped stalking the guy because I couldn't have America knowing I did shit like that.

Especially Lorne.

Chapter Ten

KIMBO SLICE

There were maybe twelve of us invited for those *SNL* auditions. It was March 2013, and Kenan Thompson—who ended up really being my home boy—had recently made headlines when he'd been misquoted by *TV Guide* talking about Black female comedians. What he actually said was "It's just a tough part of the business. Like in auditions, they just never find ones that are ready."

He didn't say no one was ready—he just said those auditions didn't help find those of us who *were* ready. But on the back of this misquote, *SNL* had decided they needed to up their game when it came to hiring women of color.

So that's why there were so many of us in New York that week to try out. There was me, LaKendra Tookes, Amber Ruffin, and later Sasheer Zamata ... and then a whole bunch of young Black sitcom actors, women who I personally didn't think were ready yet to be on *SNL*. It seemed like

Amber and I felt comfortable in the *SNL* atmosphere, but even though the others had been auditioning a lot, we got the sense these younger actresses weren't used to the kind of place *SNL* seemed to be. It is a bit intimidating, but since I was older, it didn't scare me as much.

I'm going to get in trouble for this, but I have to say it—it seemed like they wanted to be mainstream Hollywood so bad, but they didn't realize what it takes to be that: The money, the sponsorships, the support, the opportunities are different for white people, especially women. Like Chris Rock said in the foreword to this book, we don't come from the same institutions. For example, just because I'd been on BET didn't mean that anyone knew who I was. (I don't think *SNL* had the same audience as BET. And do you know how long Orange County had to fight to get BET? They had *Armenian cooking shows* before they had BET.) So, the thing they thought they were trying to be they were *not* actually being. It's way harder to be Black in Hollywood—we're already at a disadvantage. Viola Davis doesn't get to make what Meryl gets to make; we all know that.

I showed up in jeans and a T-shirt and tennis shoes— which is who I've always been—because I wanted *SNL* to know who I was. It's been my style for a long time; I'm a woman, but I don't need to always feel the need to get all dressed up to show that. As for *SNL*, I came for war. Some of the younger actresses were looking at me maybe thinking I had no class, but I didn't care—I may not be a fancy hammer, but I can hit the fuck out of a nail. They seemed to be looking at me like I wasn't the shit because of how I dressed, but I knew that I was the funniest person there.

The truth was, *SNL* didn't know what they wanted, so those girls were doing what their agents and managers told them to do. They probably didn't even know they could be themselves. It must be so hard to keep this kind of façade up, and that week, I never felt like I was really meeting these young actresses. It made me realize how far I'd come. I was lucky that I'd learned to not give a fuck, but it wasn't easy.

It's a really tough crowd at an *SNL* audition. It was exactly as you might imagine—Lorne and his producers were sitting way in the back of the completely dark theater. The folks auditioning went on, one by one, to get some kind of reaction from those shadowy figures in the back of the room. But it's a known thing in the comedy world that no one laughs during *SNL* auditions. So most of those young actresses did their auditions to silence.

But nothing fazes me. I'd been working wayyyy harder clubs than this for more than twenty years. And as soon as I got into the corridor backstage right before I was supposed to go out, I checked out the room and thought, *This is nothing different than the Comedy Store at two o'clock in the morning; hell yeah, I'm about to rip this muthafucka.*

Also I understood comedy and I know the formulas. My instincts kicked in and I knew it was the right time to do a bit. I got "lost" in the bleachers backstage; every time I was told to go straight on I'd turn right, or left.

"Chris, Chris, is it this way? Is it *this* way?"

Chris Kelly, the stage manager, would say, "I'm telling you to go straight!"

"But it don't feel right to go straight!"

"Go straight!"

"Nah, it's not right."

Everyone out in the audience could hear this, and they were already cracking up before I made it to the stage.

Out onstage, I noticed that there were empty chairs up front, and I wasn't having it.

"Nah, no way," I shouted, "that's not how it works. Everybody moves to the front—I need the energy."

I always make people move up to the front if the audience is small, whatever club I'm in. "You ain't Rosa Parks!" I say.

I couldn't give two fucks and/or a shit. And one by one, they all moved up. This was a job like any other. Whether it was true or not in my head, my confidence was saying, *They need me way more than I need them.*

I don't have characters, so I don't do characters. Instead, I just started performing. I had decided to do a build of jokes, starting as a little girl, and working my way up to present day. I began my set with a joke, saying I'd always wished I'd been Nadia Comăneci. The joke ended with me doing a cartwheel. By the end of the set I'd hit the slave joke. I said, "My name is Leslie Jones. Peace!" I put the mic back in the stand, turned around, and walked the fuck off.

I had ripped. And they were laughing.

When I came out, I had that look on my face that I knew I'd killed. Amber went in next, did the same thing, killed it, came out and said, "Yeah, that was pretty cool." I love Amber.

Then all twelve of us who had auditioned that day had to go to dinner together. I was sitting there, listening to these girls talk . . . and I was thinking, *"God, they're so young . . ."* Then my phone started going off—then LaKendra's and Amber's. We all shared a look, then we opened our phones.

"It's Jeff Blake," the texts read. He was the talent coordinator at *SNL*. "We'd like to keep you for the rest of the week so you can see the show. We want you to see how it runs."

I called the waiter over.

"Hey, is my food almost done?" I said. "Do you think you can box it up? I'm going to just go back to the hotel. I'm just so tired."

Amber said, "Me too, girl. We must be on that Cali time or something—my ass is tired!" Which is hilarious, because LA is three hours behind New York . . .

LaKendra just said, "I need to call my man."

With that, we three got our meals in boxes and left together. We walked out of that restaurant so calmly, but once we got down the block and around the corner? We went crazy, jumping around in a circle and screaming. We looked like three Laverne and Shirleys.

We all went back to my room to eat our meals and talk about what it was going to be like.

"Oh my God, we're going to meet Justin Timberlake!" I said. He was hosting that week.

"And we'll meet Kenan!" Amber said.

"Yeah, I need to ask him what he meant by us not being ready," I said, laughing.

Then, as we got more and more excited, suddenly we heard *BOOM!* Doors were slamming all over the hotel. All up and down we could hear one-sided—and very heated— conversations.

— What the fuck? This is absolutely stupid.

— I came the fuck out here and they didn't pick me. What the fuck?

— Who the fuck did they pick? Fuck SNL.

— Who they pick? We're going to find out who they picked!

"Ooh!" LaKendra said.

Amber got up like she was going to open the door to hear better.

"Don't open that door!" I whispered. "Because if you open it up, they will know and we might have to fight them bitches."

———————

I didn't think I would, but I actually loved that week at *SNL*—I had a lot to learn, and I was willing to learn it, and there were a ton of talented people there. For that week we were just there to hang out and take it all in and watch the live show on the weekend.

Kenan and I bonded immediately, too. As soon as we met, I asked him what he'd meant by us not being ready.

"First of all," Kenan said, as he closed the door, "that's not what I said. And I really hope you get this job. I told them I want someone like you here, and Lorne definitely listens to my opinion."

And that was the first moment I figured I had a shot. Before I got to *SNL*, I'd always thought sketch comics were just comics who couldn't do stand-up. But that changed after about a week of being at the table reads. I started to see that this was something I wanted to do. *I want this*, I thought. It was clear immediately how smart everyone was, how quick they were. That made me bear down—I wanted another skill, I wanted to know how to do something else. I wanted another page in my comedy portfolio.

On Saturday, we attended the live show. LaKendra, Amber, and I were sitting on one side, and in walked Sasheer from the other side. As soon as I saw her, I leaned over to LaKendra.

"That's who they going to pick," I said.

"You don't know that," LaKendra said.

"LaKendra," I said, "don't be stupid. Look at that girl. She is beautiful. Look at her teeth! And she knows how to do sketch comedy."

But I wasn't discouraged. I thought, *They might not be picking me but they might pick me as a writer. So I'm going to have to be ready to say that I'm not a writer.*

Earlier that day, I had to get an outfit for the live show and the after-party—there was nothing I could do now, so I just decided to enjoy everything. All I had at the time was a

New York & Company credit card with just $200 on it. So I found a New York & Company store, and a guy named Brian McPhatter happened to be working there—he later became my stylist and still is to this day. He put together a dope-ass outfit for me, and charged me $190.

At the party I went up to Justin Timberlake at some point and said, "Yo, dude. I kind of got beef with you. You don't know me, but I am the person that you've been stealing your moves from. I really don't appreciate that shit!"

And then I did some sweet Timberlake dance moves.

"That's my shit," I said. *"My! Shit!"* And I kept on doing his dance moves right in his face. (I was sure after that he'd want to put me in one of his videos.)

Timberlake was crying with laughter.

"You are stupid," he said.

After *SNL* I went to Indianapolis and went through that bullshit with the headliner drama I mentioned at the start of the book, and then I flew back to LA. When I got there, everything was dark, overcast.

I decided I needed my nails done.

On the way over to Fancy Nails on Adams and Crenshaw, my phone kept ringing. It was a 212 number, and I knew it meant they didn't want me, so I ignored it. But it kept ringing, on and on. *Fine, I'll answer it, get it over and done with.*

"Leslie Jones, I have Lorne Michaels for you. Please hold," a voice said.

Oh, shit. I had no idea it would be him. I thought it would be a producer.

The world was getting smaller, slower, right there in the hood. I pulled over in the parking lot of Fancy Nails, and the dark, overcast day was closing in. This was it; this was the moment. It was either the way out of the Indianapolis kind of shit, or not. But it was the moment.

"Listen, Leslie," Lorne Michaels was saying, though his words sounded as though they were underwater. "OK, I'm so sorry. We didn't pick you, but I want you to come out here and write for us."

It took me a moment to understand what he was saying. *What? Write?* That's what I was afraid of.

"Can I be honest, man?" I said, once the news had settled into my brain.

"Yes, of course," he said.

"I ain't no writer, man. I'm a performer. I'm an in-front-of-the-camera type. I'm not a behind-the-camera type. You going to bring me out there and just waste me for writing?"

Death had given me the courage. Death helped me not be scared to say my truth. There was no fucking around anymore. No one was going to tell me what to do. Everyone had died; I figured I would die, too. If they don't want no more Joneses in the world, I might as well go for it! Death gave me a new perspective. Death gave me everything.

Like I said, they needed me, but I needed them too—I needed the right platform for me. I was forty-seven, sitting in a car in the hood about to have my nails done. Nothing to lose, everything to gain. I knew how to make a way in this world, with or without *SNL*. But this sure would be nice!

"Leslie," I heard him say, as my mind spun. "I don't know what you are. But I never knew I needed you until I saw you. Just come. We'll figure it out. Just come."

"OK," I said, eventually. "But just don't make me come out there for nothing."

He laughed. "I won't," he said. We hung up, and immediately my phone rang again. It was Erik Kenward, one of the head writers.

"We need you to be out here by the seventh, so two weeks from now," he said. "We're going to give you $9,500 to move."

I hung up and I sat there for a minute. Beyond the parking lot, I could see everyone going about their day. I got out of that car, and I ran around the parking lot screaming bloody murder.

Immediately, the security guy, who knew me—I was a regular—came running over. Everyone came running out of the salon, too.

"What's wrong?" the guard shouted. "What's wrong?"

"I got *SNL*! I got *SNL*!" I screamed over and over and over again.

He looked at me puzzled. "What the fuck is *SNL*?" he said.

This is the hood. He didn't know *Saturday Night Live*—he probably thought *SNL* was slang for some kind of strange venereal disease. But from then on, he would know what *SNL* was. Leslie Fucking Jones had just gotten the job of a lifetime, and nothing would ever be the same again.

———————

I remember one day kinda asking myself, *What would I do if I had to pack up all this shit in this apartment?* With all the moves I did I collected a lot of stuff. Well, now I was about to find out. I was in the middle of a whirlwind, and I packed up everything and moved to New York.

Bear in mind I was in my mid-forties. *Fuck it, let's do it*, I thought. Even though I hadn't ever imagined this was the way I was going to take my career to the next level, maybe this *was* it. But sketch comedy? And being a writer? I wasn't sure about any of it.

One thing I knew for sure: I was going to help change the way they thought about Black female comics. I was gonna bring a new energy to the mix. I was glad I was forty-seven, though—I felt like being older meant I wouldn't be so at risk from the kind of politics I'd been warned about that got played at *SNL*. In my mind, I wasn't a young comic trying to make a career—I was gonna play it like Michael Corleone.

Things didn't start out well at all. Even though I'd been hired as a writer, nothing I was pitching was being picked for the show. I'd told Lorne in that first phone call to not bring me out to New York for no reason—"just don't make me come out there for nothing," I'd said—but here I was, nothing to show for weeks of work. I wasn't in front of the camera and my sketches weren't being chosen, so what the fuck *was* I doing in New York? It's not an easy place to live. I was frustrated because I wanted to win now! At this point, though, I was more like Fredo Corleone.

Coming up with sketches was a nightmare. Writing is difficult and personal, and I couldn't work out how to transfer my jokes to sketches. With the sketch, you have to set up a background and have other people participating. It was so hard for me at first. I wasn't giving myself any grace and I wasn't giving credit to the fact there was a system, a formula I had not learned yet.

I remember talking to Steve Higgins about it. Steve had started at *SNL* back in 1995, and by the time I got there he was a producer and writer on the show.

"I'm bombing, Steve," I said one Wednesday night after another one of my sketches hadn't been picked. "And I *don't* bomb."

"Go home," Steve said. "Eat something. You'll be fine." This was back when I thought me and Steve were cool. And I believe we were, but down the line that changed. Later, I came to feel that he thought I was a hack-ass comic who got lucky and didn't appreciate where I was. But plenty of people have doubted me, and I've been fine.

One of my first sketch pitches was the moment I learned that pitching was something I had to work at. Usually I'm good at selling ideas, but pitching sketches is an art.

I wrote and pitched a sketch to Melissa McCarthy. It was the sketch version of a joke I had been doing which I'd nicknamed "Big Women in the House." When I'm onstage I refer to myself as a "big bitch." For *SNL*, I changed it to "real women" because essentially that is what I meant.

For the sketch, Melissa and I would be talking to some guy in a club: "You're out there in this club trying to get these skinny pretty bitches? You know, when you go to her house, she ain't going to have no food in her refrigerator, right? Me, I got a whole meat loaf and some mashed potatoes, some biscuits and string beans! I got two parking spots. You ain't gotta park on the street, boo. Ain't going to be no ticket for you. Look at my TV! I got a Samsung Series 6—you know how many esses is in that? I'm just going hand you the remote—you got all the power in my house."

I even created a jingle for it: "Real women got real curves, real women got real swerves!" The whole point was, we may be bigger than skinny bitches, but we're the size that women really are—those skinny bitches are starving! You're not supposed to be a size zero. But Melissa really wasn't feeling it.

I had the biggest lump in my throat. OMG—did I not explain it right? I was horrified. The truth was, something I always kill at—being funny—I wasn't killing at in the early days at *SNL*. I found myself crying from frustration and anger, and Michael Che came and talked to me.

"Do you know how many times you're going to have to pitch to people?" he said. "You're going to need a thicker skin."

Later that week at the Saturday night after-party (it was, coincidentally, also Seth Meyers's leaving party), Melissa came up to me.

"I just want to tell you that sketch wasn't for me—you wrote that sketch for *you*," she said. "That is really a *you* sketch—*you* should be doing that sketch."

"Well, babe," I said, "I'm not a cast member or a host. So, what do I do now?"

"Well," she said, "I'm just letting you know. I didn't want to hurt your feelings."

"You didn't hurt my feelings," I said, "but I did want to fight you, though." Thank God she laughed at that because I just wanted to make her laugh. And then she hugged me.

———————

None of this was getting my stuff on *SNL*, though. I wasn't in full respect mode yet. I wasn't respecting how *SNL* works, and it doesn't matter how funny you are, you still need to humble yourself to the process. Trying to fit into a system I was never going to fit into—I had to think of it as I'm a passenger on a train, not the train. I need to just take the ride. I still had to figure out where I could fit in. I was in New York, in a dream job, but I was just spinning my wheels.

Before the end of the first season, I was done—I figured this *SNL* shit wasn't going to work out. I didn't even want to show up anymore, but luckily, Taran Killam took me to one side.

"You can't give up," Taran said. "They're training you right now, getting you ready for Weekend Update. This is just the shit that they going to make you do."

"Well, I'm too old for this shit," I said. "I'm not a child." But what I didn't get was that I had great ideas, I just had not learned how to sell them.

None of my own writing was being used; all I'd do was write and then go home. I was just happy if something made it to the table read. I'd sometimes write with someone else; I still have the file of all the ideas I had. One of them was about Jesus having a PR person—"you can't wear those sandals now; they're made out of real animals . . ." But it never got picked up. I think I was trying to write like the *SNL* writers, in their style of humor, but that wasn't gonna work. I had to figure out my lane. I still wasn't a cast member yet, either, so I was worried.

I went and found Lindsay Shookus, a producer, to talk to her about it.

"I know you're having trouble," Lindsay said, "but we're trying to get you ready for Update."

"Why does everyone keep saying that? I'm *ready!*" I said. I was just so ready to get into the game, to show them what I had. I wanted to show them I could do it.

Six months after I'd started, one Tuesday night Higgins, and one of the producers, Erin Doyle, called me.

"We want you to do an Update," Higgins said.

Finally!

I already had two jokes ready to go—the slave joke I'd used in my audition, and a texting joke. They told me they wanted me to combine the two, but I told them it wouldn't have worked. First, the texting joke is not a joke you can make into an Update, and they are two different jokes anyway—they don't go together. In the end I asked them which one they wanted, and they picked the slave joke, and they sent me off to work with the Update team to fine-tune it.

Problem was, the Update team worked on my slave joke, but their job is to flesh a joke out. Since this was my first Update, of course I was going to follow the routine, so I took the joke to rehearsal and used what they'd written.

It didn't work because it wasn't me and with all the added stuff the joke changed.

There was a sad liberation in not having family, in having been through what I'd been through. When you've lost so much you're not afraid of speaking up and saying something isn't gonna work. I had tried it their way, now it was time to try mine.

"You guys don't get me yet," I said. "I know you got a system, but I'm telling you it's not the joke, and it's not gonna work like that."

Thank God for Bryan Tucker. He was the head writer at the time. (He ended up being the one who always wrote for me.) I told him what was going on.

"OK," Bryan said, "just go in that room over there with Che and write the joke word for word, exactly how you do it onstage."

So that's what we did—me and Che sat down, and we wrote that bit, word for word, and put it on the cue cards. Then we took it to the dress show (the show on Saturday evening before the live one) . . . and it *destroyed* so hard to the point where everybody was saying that it was going to be an unforgettable Update. (This was also the Update where I would first call Colin Jost "a delectable Caucasian" and set in motion our long-standing flirtation.)

I was psyched, but then Lorne Michaels made sure I didn't get too ahead of myself. He took me into his office.

"You did really good in the dress," Lorne said, "but don't get happy. Don't celebrate. When you do a good live, *that's* when you can celebrate. Now, go out there and do it the same way and kill."

I was a basketball player—I react to shit like that. I'm competitive. I love a good coach, and that was just what I needed to hear. I thought about how I used to react to Coach Berger: *I can hype the fuck outta shit. There's something in me that can get people so fired up, just by being me. I can even feel that energy leave my body; I can feel people get it. They are pumped; it's like an aerosol or something that I shoot out. No one is going to fuck with me.* That's what it felt like; by the time I walked out of his office, I knew I was going to rip that muthafucka.

Sure enough, that night—Saturday May 3, 2014—I went out there and I killed.

The way we view Black beauty has changed . . . I'm single right now, but back in the slave days, I would have never been single. I'm six feet tall and I'm strong . . . Look at me, I'm a Mandingo . . . I do not want to be a slave. Hell, I don't like working for you white people now, and y'all pay me . . . back in the slave days, my love life would have been way better. Master would have hooked me up with the best brotha on the plantation, and every nine months I'd be in the corner having a super baby . . . I'd just be in the corner popping them out. Shaq. Kobe. LeBron. Kimbo Slice. Sinbad . . . I would be the number one slave draft pick. All of the plantations would want me . . . Now, I can't even get a

brotha to take me out for a cheap dinner. I mean,
damn, can a bitch get a beef bowl?

Not surprisingly, a bunch of folks hiding behind their
keyboards thought it was offensive—some even got upset
about it being a "rape" joke, when there's nothing whatso-
ever to do with rape in it. "This Leslie Jones person is an
embarrassment," someone from *Ebony* magazine wrote in a
tweet. "I'm so appalled right now." It was interesting that she
and others never went after Key and Peele for their "Auction
Block" sketch on Comedy Central—that, too, was about
slavery, their two characters upset that no one bought them
at auction. But then, they're men, so . . .

I had to go on Twitter to defend myself—over a series of
tweets that following Sunday I wrote this:

Y'all so busy trying to be self righteous you miss what
the joke really is. Very sad I have to defend myself to
black people. Now I'm betting if Chris Rock or Dave
[Chappelle] did that joke or jay z or Kanye put in a
rap they would be called brilliant. Cause they all do
this type of material. Just cause it came from a strong
black woman who ain't afraid to be real y'all mad. So
here is my announcement, black folks, you won't stop
me and [I'm] gonna go even harder and deeper now.
Cause it's a shame that we kill each other instead of
support each other. This exactly why black people are
where we are now. I wouldn't be able to do a joke like
that if I didn't know my history or [wasn't] proud of

where I came from and who I am. My dad is the big-
gest militant in the world and he would have loved that
joke. My grandmother went to jail for whooping two
white men asses for attacking her she was also 6'2 and
strong. And she laughed her ass off. Get over yourself
and you might as well get [used] to it cause I'm good
at what I do and I ain't going NOWHERE!!!

Fortunately, I got backup from smart people like Rox-
ane Gay, who wrote, "I have watched the clip several times
now. Beyond the surface of the joke, I see pain. I see rage. I
see a woman speaking her truth."

That ridiculous backlash that came after hit me in so
many different ways. I had done this joke in Black clubs and
white clubs for six years, so I didn't understand why now. It
amazes me how people interpret shit.

During the live show that night I came off the stage, and
Lorne was waiting by the door. He hugged me.

Lorne Michaels is not a hugger, but he was a hugger with
me. I hugged him all the time—I would grab him and literally body slam him in the middle of the hallway. He loved it.
Everybody was scared of him, except for me. If you go back
and look at the "Leslie Wants to Play Trump" sketch, Lorne
even agreed to having me throw him around in his office.
Folks would see him walk through the hallways and would
run, and I would be screaming *"Lorne!"* and then I would
run and grab him and shake him.

I was not going to take *SNL* for granted. For me it was
like I'd finally made it to the majors. "We're playing

baseball, right? And every Saturday too?" I think I brought a breath of fresh air in with that attitude, and woke people up a bit. Partly I had that attitude because I was the oldest on the cast, and partly it was because of what I'd been through. After my brother died, I just abused myself. I dated terrible guys, did all kinds of stupid shit. I thought, *The world has killed everybody anyway* . . . In a way, *SNL* kind of saved me a little bit (as did a really great new therapist in New York)—I had work to do, so I just did it.

———————

By the time of that first Update, I still wasn't a cast member—still just a writer. I figured nothing was going to make me a cast member if that Update didn't seal the deal. Bryan Tucker eventually told me that they didn't want to make me a cast member, but they did want to offer me six Updates.

"They want me to live in New York to come in and do six Updates?" I couldn't believe it—they didn't even want me to keep writing—just six Updates. I was crushed.

While all this was happening, Lorne had gotten me cast in a Zach Galifianakis movie, *Masterminds*, during the summertime, so he knew I could kill a role and he knew I was a hustler, but still no movement on being a cast member. It made no sense. Everybody wanted me at this point. HBO was interested; *Two Broke Girls* wanted me to be a character on their show, too. It felt like everyone was coming out of the woodwork—and it was just me and a manager handling all the requests—and still *SNL* wasn't going to put me in front of the camera except for once in a while on the Update desk. I took this as a challenge.

When *SNL* reconvened in the fall of 2014, I wanted to show them I was undeniable. Yes, I needed them, but they needed me, too. No one else can be Leslie Fucking Jones. I wanted them to see that I knew who I was, and why I was there. And the way to do that, I figured, was to show them what *SNL* would feel like when I'm not there.

That first week I went in, did the regular Leslie thing, brought all the excitement. They'd written a sketch for Chris Pratt, the host, about football players and the crimes they'd committed. Kenan's character, Kendrick Douglas, says, "I hit my wife," and then it cut to me, Mrs. Kendrick Douglas: "And I'm his wife—I hit his ass back!"

It killed, just as my Update about being single had ("Are you single? Are you on drugs? Are you gay? Are you sure? Do you have any kids—the baby on the way counts as a baby . . .").

Also that week, I remember Che saying, "They don't see what I see. I'm going to put you in a sketch so they *can* see."

"Yes! *I'll* make them hire me," I said. I believe that ninety-nine-cent video was a big part of me getting cast, too.

My plan was very simple: only show up on the weeks I had an Update. I really wanted them to see what it felt like when my energy wasn't in the building. I didn't show up for the pitch, though I did show up for the table read because they had a line for me. I did the line, then raised my hand like I was in church and just left. Then, I skipped rehearsal; I just showed up for the live show on Saturday evening. When I arrived that night, I was walking down the hall and ran right into Lorne.

"Where have you been?" he said. "Where's my star been?"

"I'm your *star*? How am I your star? I'm not a cast member," I said, laughing.

That night, at the after-party, something miraculous happened. I was talking to Higgins when a guy from HBO walked by.

"We're interested, Leslie," he said.

"Listen, man, now's not the time," I said, laughing.

A few minutes later, one of the girls from *Two Broke Girls* also walked by.

"We wrote you a part!" she said, without me having to say a word. Though they didn't know it, these people were like more angels sent to nudge the universe in my direction. I wish I could say that I'd organized that shit, but I hadn't— the universe just gave it to me.

But as ever, nothing comes without a fight. Next day I got a call from my lawyer.

"*SNL* is now saying that you have to show up for the pitches, you need to be at the table reads, and you need to be at the shows."

"No!" I said. "That's all for cast members. They only asked me to do six Updates, remember?"

I told my manager at the time to contact Lauren Roseman and tell them that it had been an incredible experience, but I was not to be put on the shelf. They couldn't just take my time up like that. So many people want me, and if they're not making me a cast member, I can't stay here and just do six Updates. I'd rather go back to LA and try my thing there.

I thought, *I sure hope this works*, but you either believe in yourself or you don't. I'm not desperate; I have a talent. And I'm a business.

A few days later, my manager got back to me.

"Next week is Jim Carrey. They asked if you could join for pitch."

So, I went to the meeting to pitch Jim Carrey, and while I was there, Lorne Michaels asked to see me.

I went to his office, and he was standing there in his beautiful, sky blue, cashmere sweater.

"We are just going to go ahead and make you a cast member," he said. "I don't want you to go win the Super Bowl somewhere else."

"You know I'm about to show my ass now, right?" I said, laughing.

"I know," he said, wearily. And then I hugged him.

Then things got even more amazing.

The very next night I took a meeting with movie director Paul Feig. He'd seen me do the slave joke on Update, and apparently he'd made a note of it, just like everyone else. Paul wanted a meeting, so I went to see him in Manhattan; during that meeting, he offered me a part in his remake of *Ghostbusters*.

I remember I was wearing a super cute outfit, and it was a beautiful night, one of those evenings where the air is clear and there's an energy to the streets that you can't find anywhere else but New York City. I left that meeting and I was walking down Fifth Avenue. In my head the Bee Gees' "Stayin' Alive" was playing as I strutted along.

I'd just been made cast member on *SNL*; I was going to star in a huge Hollywood movie. As I strutted along to Barry Gibb's falsetto in my head, I remember looking at all the people walking along Fifth Avenue. I got to a "don't walk" sign, and I waited with the crowd. I looked around at every one of them all just going about their evenings in that amazing city, and I was thinking, *You don't even know how big I'm about to blow up, muthafuckas . . .*

Chapter Eleven

WHO YA GONNA CALL?

"I don't like this movie," the journalist said, "and you've got five minutes to prove to me that it is worth watching."

The cast of *Ghostbusters* was on a press junket somewhere in Europe, and some guy with a German or Scandinavian or Russian accent or whatever had just had the balls to say that the movie we'd just made wasn't "worth it," and that we owed him an explanation.

Ghostbusters came out July 11, 2016, but before it had even hit the movie theaters it had been the subject of intense online abuse—and no surprise that I was the one who got most of the hate. For a start, sad keyboard warriors living in their mothers' basements hated the fact that this hallowed work of perfect art now featured—gasp! horror!—women in the lead roles. Worst of all, of course, was that one of the lead characters was a Black woman. For some men this was the final straw.

It wasn't just racism and misogyny, either. A lot of it had to do with the fact that I was playing an MTA worker, as though that was something I should be ashamed of. I'd tried to fight back— I was a comic—I was used to someone heckling me, so for every piece of bullshit on Twitter I had a reply:

> *"If they made me a scientist you would be mad at what type of scientist. Seriously it's a f—king movie get over yourself."*
>
> *"You haven't seen the movie yet you don't know wtf my char is. you [go] by a trailer. omg are y'all that arrogant. So is [an] MTA worker trash?"*
>
> *"Why can't a regular person be a Ghostbuster?*
>
> *"Regular People save the world everyday so if I'm the stereotype!! Then so be it!! We walk among Heroes and take them for granted. IT'S NOT A MAN, WOMAN, RACE, CLASS THANG!! ITS A GHOSTBUSTER THANG!! AND AS FAR AS IM CONCERNED WE ALL GHOSTBUSTERS!! STAND TALL!!"*

Eight days after the movie premiered, I took my Twitter account down so we could work out who was trying to hack me (there had been multiple attempts to hack me by this point). And there had been so much racist abuse that I had no choice. I wrote,

> *I leave Twitter tonight with tears and a very sad heart. All this 'cause I did a movie. You can hate the movie but the shit I got today . . . wrong.*

Earlier that same evening I'd gotten a tweet from Jack Dorsey, then CEO of Twitter, telling me to DM him. He was aware that I was being brutally attacked with racial slurs and worse, and started putting people on my account—this was basically the start of Twitter taking this shit more seriously. (Jack put people on my account to monitor it because someone is *always* trying to hack me; it's a daily occurrence—but with Musk, who knows? Either way, I have my own security on that account now.)

People made such a big deal of the fact of me taking my account down rather than *why* I had to take it down. It was simple: I was shutting it down temporarily while working out what to do with all these muthafuckas hitting me; and anyway, it was back up the next day.

That night of July 18 was horrible, though. I remember crying and thinking, *This is the first time I had ever seen it so bad. How do y'all all get together to bully a person?* It wasn't as if I'd committed a crime or something—I was being bullied over a movie, over playing a part in a movie. (I can't believe I have to say this out loud.)

The weakness of muthafuckas amazes me. I cried not because I was being bullied, but because this is our world and because I can't believe anyone would do this shit to someone, anyone, for *working*. This is awful. I am in a *movie*. Death threats for something as small as that? The world was not as rosy as I'd hoped it was. But none of that shit was about me.

But then that same night Kate McKinnon came over, we drank some wine, and I went on about my business.

Of all the women in Paul's remake of the movie, I was the one who got taken through the ringer. I wonder why . . . Oh, right, because I was a Black girl. I was being sent films of being hanged, of white guys jacking off on my picture, saying, "You fucking nigger. We going to kill you." Why are people being so evil to each other? How can you sit and type "I want to kill you." Who does that?

And it wasn't just racist shit, either—when I started doing this movie, this is when I really started seeing not only racism, but classism. Even the director of *Ghostbusters: Afterlife*, Jason Reitman—who is the son of the original director, Ivan—said something unforgivable when discussing his new version that came out in 2021. On Bill Burr's podcast he said this about our version of *Ghostbusters*:

> *We are, in every way, trying to go back to the original technique and hand the movie back to the fans.*

He did try to walk it back, tweeting,

> *Wo, that came out wrong! I have nothing but admiration for Paul and Leslie and Kate and Melissa and Kristen and the bravery with which they made* Ghostbusters 2016. *They expanded the universe and made an amazing movie!*

But the damage was done. Bringing up the idea of giving the movie "back to the fans" was a pretty clear shout-out to all those losers who went after us for making an all-female film. It was made clear to me at times during the process that I was lucky to even be on that movie, but honestly, I was thinking, *I don't have to be in this muthafucka* . . . Especially as I got paid way less than Melissa McCarthy and Kristen Wiig. No knock on them, but my first offer was to do that movie for $67,000. I had to fight to get more (in the end I got $150K), but the message was clear: "This is gonna blow you up—after this, you're made for life," all that kind of shit, as though I hadn't had decades of a successful career already. And in the end, all it made for me was heartache and one big-ass controversy.

Fortunately, I learned a lot from Melissa on that shoot. If she looked at a shot and she didn't think it was right, she'd suggest that it be shot from a different side or angle. Back then I didn't know you could change your shots until I saw Melissa and Kristen do it. And these days I do the same kinds of things that they did on *Ghostbusters.*

But listen, I had a great time, too. I bonded with Kate. I loved Boston, became a kind of Bostonian. We were right by Fenway. We'd walk from the set through a beautiful park to the hotel. People would recognize us, come by to say hi. I loved that city. And being trained to do, and then doing, the stunts themselves? I loved that. And the crew was fucking incredible, too, really sweet and helpful. (I recently did a shoot in Boston and some of the crew talked about making *Ghostbusters.* They all had great memories, which helped me see the positives, too.)

I think that's why one of the worst things about that movie is that it should have been a great film. That crew deserved for y'all to see the movie we actually made. But a lot of stuff got cut for cost.

What no one realizes to this day is that me and Kate had some great moments that you didn't get to see. There were moments with Melissa and Kristen that got cut, too, that I thought were important in explaining how their friendship came to be in the movie. If they had released the movie as we'd shot it, I swear things would have been different. Paul Feig was awesome during the shooting, and we were doing improv all over the place, and there was even a dance scene that was so dope. Michael Williams, God rest his soul, choreographed a scene where Chris Hemsworth was possessed and took over the whole army. It was like a really funny, weird version of "Thriller"—Chris was standing on top of a movie theater dancing, while Michael Williams was in the front of all the FBI agents and soldiers on the ground, just killing it. It was the best thing. The day of that taping we were so excited because we figured that when people saw this, they were going to *lose* it.

Nope—it got cut. The reason given was that the special effects needed were too expensive, or some bullshit. But if this film can't afford special effects, then what the fuck are we doing making a *Ghostbusters* movie in the first place? Then there was a fight scene I shot that also got cut.

When they later announced the Jason Reitman version, *Afterlife*, which completely ignored the fact that there had been an all-female version, and all that "giving it back to the fans" shit, I could not stay quiet; I had to say something. I wrote on Twitter,

So insulting. Like, fuck us. We dint count. It's like some-
thing trump would do. (Trump voice) "Gonna redo
ghostbusteeeeers, better with men, will be huge. Those
women ain't ghostbusteeeeers" ugh so annoying. Such a
dick move. And I don't give a fuck I'm saying something!!

Turns out that excitement I felt walking down Fifth Avenue after my meeting with Paul Feig? It morphed into a
learning experience, but parts of it were really painful, too.

But maybe something good came out of all this after
all—by the end of that shoot, I knew so much more than I
did when I started. By the end I was thinking, *This shit won't*
ever happen again. I know that I'm not a big star yet, but after
this muthafucka, after figuring this out, I'm about to release
the Kraken.

Why would the world be so against a female
Ghostbusters—it's iconic! What does that say about
everyone? I think if we'd made it now, things might—*might*—
be different, who knows. (Oh, no—I forgot about the
reaction to the Black mermaid . . .)

And that foreign journalist who asked us to justify the
movie to him?

"I've been so good at doing press today. I did twenty-two
interviews!" I said to Melissa and Kristen and Kate and
Lauren Roseman, the publicist, after they told me about the
foreign journalist's bitch-ass question. "Y'all didn't let me at
him? I deserve that. You didn't let me get in a room with him
and *A Bronx Tale* his ass? I would have locked the door and
said, 'Now, youse can't leave, muthafucka.'"

———————

Before I could go back to *SNL*, though, and use what I'd learned about how to stick up for myself as a star, more shit hit the fan.

Around that time, I had been talking to someone on Match.com, and the thing is, I thought I was talking to the man of my dreams. This is why I understand and have sympathy for stuff that women do online. I was talking to him, and I sent him nudes. Not my proudest moment, but I will say they were excellent nudes. I mean, I looked amazing—that's why I sent them.

But there was always a reason this guy couldn't come to see me—it got to the point where I even said, "You're never coming back to New York? You said you lived here once . . . You haven't even FaceTimed with me." He kept saying that he was in Italy somewhere, taking care of his mom. The whole time Taran Killam was telling me, "Leslie, this is a catfish," but I kept saying I believed it—no way it was a catfish. I wasn't that stupid, and anyway, I'd never even heard the word catfishing.

Eventually, I called the man of my dreams out on his lack of commitment to coming to New York; I told him I was done with his games and that I didn't think he was a real person.

And that's when he said, "Well, OK. If you're not gonna talk to me anymore, then I'm going to release your nudes, Miss Ghostbuster. So, you better gimme $20,000."

Taran was right—I was being catfished.

The first thing I thought was, *This is Match.com? Y'all supposed to protect me!* I reached out to them, but what were they going to do apart from suspend the account? Every time that Match.com commercial came on, I'd be thinking, *Fuck you, muthafucka. Fuck your old ass. You don't know that this catfish is fucking this bitch's life up. Put that in your commercial, old man.*

That's when the authorities got involved. I was supposed to get this catfish—who turned out to be a ring of losers, so not exactly the man of my dreams—on the phone so they could record me being threatened. My job was to keep the person on the line long enough to maybe trace where he was calling from. The woman from the DA's office said, "I need you to do your best acting."

So even though I was indignant as fuck, I figured, *I'm an actor, I got this.*

I got the guy on the phone. He started talking shit.

"You need to send me the money, because I'm gonna release the nudes."

"Right, alright," I said, "so who do I need to send it to? You need to send me the information. And how do I know for sure that you're gonna not show the nudes?"

At this, the muthafucka turned so slimy and disgusting.

"Here's where you can send it," he said, giving me the details, "and you know what? You know what? Now that I'm thinking about it, you need to gimme $35,000."

That was it—I lost it.

"What?!" I screamed. "You're not gonna get shit, you piece of shit muthafucka." I was yelling everything I could think of. There was a click; the call had ended.

The DA put her head in her hands and whispered, "I thought you were an actor."

"Did you hear him?" I said, indignantly.

"But you knew he was going to do that," she said. "Anyway, we'll take what we've got and try to figure it out."

Unfortunately, this is where the FBI got involved. They made me email them the photos so they could know what they were dealing with (later, Homeland Security would get involved and they said the FBI should have just taken my computer). But none of my shit was protected, and emailing the pictures to the FBI turned out to be a terrible idea.

I was in the middle of the *Ghostbusters* shit—it was a month after the movie came out—and the hackers were all over me, and they got everything. The morning after I'd emailed the stuff to the FBI I was woken by a phone call. I looked at the number—818 area code? No idea.

"Who is this?" I said.

"I'm from TMZ," she said. "Do you know that your nudes and your passport and your ID and everything else is up online?"

They'd gotten it all from old emails.

I couldn't believe what I was hearing.

"What?"

"Yeah," she said, "they just revealed it. What do you have to say about that?"

"How did you get this number? Did you get it from the hacking?"

"I was trying to help."

"You're not helping, you fucking bitch," I yelled, and hung up.

My then publicist, Lauren Roseman—one of the best publicists—called me, and had that shit down and off the internet in fifteen minutes, but still, fifteen minutes is fifteen hours in the internet world.

Needless to say, it was painfully ironic that ring of small dicks didn't leak the nudes after all—just some evil hacker had done it because the FBI had had me email them.

That day, I remember sitting on the couch thinking, *If I was twenty-seven, this shit would be fucking me up right now.* But when it happened, I was forty-eight and a soldier. Did they think that they were going to computer-scare me? I'm not going to lie—it hurt for a second, because it was absolute evil. We have evil people in the world, and this is a sure sign of it, and it's terrifying that people can behave this way. But I know I haven't done anything wrong. Yes, I will have to explain to my aunt why my vagina is all over the internet, but these photographs are my personal property, as is my vagina.

As for the *Ghostbusters* abuse, that too was terrifying because again, people don't realize it's not real life. I know all too well about racism, but this kind of abuse was next level.

And even with the hacking, people close to me let me down. I had a lawyer at the time who counseled me that I should put myself across as the victim in all of this.

I fired him for that—no way was I a victim. I sent those nudes. I'm not a victim. Somebody hacked into my account, my personal account, and went through my shit. That's against the law; that's a crime. But no, I'm no victim—you can kiss my dick.

I sent those nudes, and what do comedians do when something bad happens? We take all the bad shit, and we make it into a joke.

And that's what I did—I went right ahead and did two things to own it.

First, on the Emmy broadcast on September 18, I did a bit with the Ernst and Young guys who came onstage to talk about how they safeguard the vote tallies.

"Let's be real," I said. "Y'all protecting something that nobody is trying to steal. Don't nobody want to know about Emmy secrets. But since you good at keeping things safe, I got a job for you. My Twitter account! Put that in a vault please! Y'all over here using your skills to protect Best Voiceover in a French Sitcom, meanwhile I'm over here butt naked on CNN! I just wanted to feel beautiful, y'all."

An *SNL* producer had seen a version of this bit before it aired and had taken me to one side to urge me to not say that last part about wanting to feel beautiful.

"You don't need it," she said.

"*You* don't need it," I said. "But *I* do."

That night I remember Trevor Noah coming up to me and saying, "You are literally my hero right now. That was just exactly how you take your power back."

I was honest with Trevor.

LESLIE F*CKING JONES   219

"This hiding shit? Becoming a victim shit? It doesn't really work. And it doesn't make shit fade away." By owning it at the Emmys, the message I was sending was *I'm not scared. I was built for hard.*

Then I doubled down by writing an *SNL* Update about the whole thing.

"I was recently hacked myself," I said. "All they did was release nude pics of me, which is nothing because I don't know if you know this about me, but I ain't shy . . . I am very comfortable with who I am. I am an open book. I keep my porn in a folder labeled 'PORN.' If you want to see Leslie Jones naked, just *ask* . . . You can't embarrass me more than I have embarrassed myself . . . At a certain point, you stop being embarrassed and start being you. And I have been me for forty-nine years . . . The only person who can hack me is me."

With these two bits—the Emmys and the Update—I was planting a seed. I was saying "It's mine, now." When I said "If you wanted to see my nudes, all you had to do was *ask*," I was proving that Leslie Jones knows how to take care of herself.

Everything had changed once again. I had a new coat of armor. No one was going to fuck with me again. Everybody was about to find out.

Chapter Twelve

KILLING WHOOPI GOLDBERG

The process of *SNL*, and what I learned there, was so valuable. A typical week at *SNL* goes like this:

Sunday is the only day off; after the stress of the live show on Saturday night, everyone is exhausted. There was a rule I learned the first season—no matter how upset you are, just wait until Monday. Everyone is emotional and beat and it's not a good time to yell at folks. I don't know if I followed that rule during the first season, but I did learn to eventually! But you're right back to it Monday, which is pitch day. You go in around five or six in the evening, meet that week's host, and pitch stuff to them—it's not material that's necessarily going to be on the show; instead it's really to make them feel comfortable and to make them laugh and trust us, and know that we trust them and will involve them.

Sometimes stuff from that pitch does get written, but not always.

On Mondays I would stay behind with Kenan and I'd smoke and sometimes we'd talk to writers about sketches we wanted to write.

Tuesday is the night guts are busted, when there are all kinds of hopes and dreams and wonderful things that you think are going to happen for the show. We all hang out in our offices, and the host goes to each writer's room and lets us pitch to them. "Are you interested in this? Are you interested in that?" Once we settled on something, then the fun kicks in—we'd just write. I remember that Kenan and I would come up with ideas that became sketches, though for some of them I'd just end up saying "Nah, I'm just high."

When I first started at *SNL*, on Tuesdays I would show up right at noon or one p.m., but then I realized we'd be there till three or four in the morning. Kenan told me I could come in later. I started to come in at five, and the rule Kenan made was we always left at midnight. "There are sixteen writers," he'd say. "They're supposed to be writing the whole show. Not you." But those Tuesdays . . . man, sometimes we'd just kick it and I'd smoke weed and we'd laugh so hard, and write funny stuff from that.

For example, there was this one week I was going to get Whoopi to sit in on the Update desk. (I'd played her on the show a few times because I was the closest looking to her. Kenan used to play her, too, but he was sick of dressing as a Black woman—it's one of the reasons they started looking for a Black woman to join the cast.)

Anyway, in the sketch, Colin would say, "Leslie, I know it's you," and Whoopi would say, "No, no, I know Leslie plays me, but it's really me, I'm really Whoopi."

Colin then says, "Yeah, yeah. So what would happen if I do this?" and pulls out a gun.

Whoopi looks terrified.

"Yo, no, seriously, I'm Whoopi Goldberg . . . I'm not Leslie, I'm really Whoopi . . ."

Colin looks at her, doesn't believe her, says, "Oh yeah . . ."

And then shoots her.

Then it was going to get even better. In the old days of TV if something went wrong, or they had a station break, they'd cut to a pre-taped picture, and I had so much fun imagining what we could show right after Colin shot Whoopi: we'd show maybe an even shorter version of Lorne on a moped, Lorne taking a shower, Lorne playing golf, Lorne riding a horse. And Lorne in a voiceover would be saying, "We'll be right back, baby . . ."

Then we go back and Che is screaming, "Colin, why did you shoot Whoopi Goldberg??? Oh my God!"

Then back to the station break, more little Lorne riding something.

Then back to *SNL*:

"Oh my god, I'm losing a lot of blood," whimpers Whoopi.

People are running around in horror.

"You shot Whoopi Goldberg!" Lorne screams.

Kenan and I were weeping with laughter when we wrote this—we were actually going to shoot Whoopi Goldberg on *SNL*!

We went to pitch it to Bryan Tucker: "We've got to write this Update. This has got to happen!"

Tucker just looked at us blankly.

"You want to shoot Whoopi Goldberg on national TV?" he said. "You guys are crazy."

"Tucker, you don't get it!" I said. "We're gonna take it to the Update team."

"Fine," he said, "I have seventeen sketches to write. Please get out of my office."

In the Update office we were acting the Whoopi sketch out and laughing the whole time. When we finished, Kenan said, "It's so funny. Right?"

"You guys are nuts," someone said. "You can't kill Whoopi Goldberg on live TV . . ."

"She's not dead!" I shouted. "She just got shot."

I think they could tell that we were serious. Someone said, "Just write it . . ."

So we did—we wrote that sketch and brought it to the table read, which is what Wednesdays are all about at *SNL*.

When it came to the station break stuff, we even got Lorne to read the voiceover, which was hysterical. But then he stopped it.

"We're not going to kill Whoopi Goldberg on national TV for a personal joke," he said, completely missing the point but it was hilarious when he said it. It wasn't an inside joke at all—it was just funny. But we never got to do it. (I later told Whoopi about it, and she thought it was hysterical . . . and she said for sure she would have done the sketch if we'd asked her to.)

Wednesday's table reads are supposed to start at around three thirty or four, but it never got going before five because that's around when Lorne gets in. We'd read about thirty -eight to forty sketches around the table, written by everyone, and then they—meaning Lorne, Higgins, Colin, Che, Tucker, the other head writers—would all head off to Lorne's office to pick maybe twelve. Those twelve tended to make it to the dress rehearsal, but only around six would usually survive to the actual show. This cutting of sketches from forty to six led to us referring to the day as Ash Wednesday, because all the dreams you had on Tuesday? They'd be pretty much dead twenty-four hours later.

Whoever gets their sketches picked sticks around to talk to the director and the hair and makeup and set people, all to get the sketch ready. Thursday and Friday tend to be the pre-tape days, and they'd sometimes keep you till three or four in the morning; by the time I left, they did get a little tighter with that schedule.

Friday is also rehearsal day, all leading up to Saturday, where we'd do three shows: rehearsal, dress with one crowd, then the actual live show with a whole new crowd. To me, the dress was the best show to see, because that crowd gets to see all the sketches including the ones that get cut for the live show.

Not everything goes well during the live show, either, let me tell you.

My first season, I was the worst with the cue cards—the *worst*. The cards are color coded, but at the start I couldn't for the life of me work out which was mine. Thank God for Chris Kelly, one of the stage managers—if I could, I'd have him be my stage manager on everything forever. I love that man. I'd be shouting, "What color am I? I can't see the card. Which card is mine? That's not my camera, Chris. Which one is my camera?" and Chris would just calmly say, "This is your line" or "Here, this is your camera." Sometimes Cecily Strong and Kenan would fuck with me and point to the wrong camera, and Chris would get so mad at them: "Don't do that to her—you know she'll do what you say!" We'd be rehearsing and I would be facing the wrong way and all you could see in the camera was my ears; Cecily and Kenan would be dying of laughter which would make me start laughing, too.

Kenan and Cecily are my hearts. It's funny to me, too, because Cecily and I did not start off like that. I went out with her and some of her friends one night, and she was teasing one friend so hard. And, of course, the little girl that protects people came out. I said, "Why you doing her like that?" But Cecily didn't miss a beat because if you know her, you know she loves her friends. "That's how I am with my friends—it's not serious, Leslie!" she said. And then she started imitating me in a way that to this day I bust out laughing just thinking about. (One of the things I learned at *SNL* is that everyone is funny.) Eventually Cecily and I ended up on a trip together and we realized that we are so similar. I love that woman. We don't even talk all the time anymore, but when we do, it's like we've been talking to each other all the time. That girl is talented as fuck! And she, along with Kenan, were the rocks that made *SNL* work.

But even Cecily couldn't save me from the Chris Rock sketch "The Arguing Couple." This was the first time I was in a sketch by myself with just the host, and Chris worked hard to make me the star of it. It had gone fine in dress—perfect, in fact. But between dress and the live show some lines had changed, some positions, and they didn't go through it with us, and I was lost. I had no idea what color I was supposed to be looking for on the cue cards—blue, black, no idea (the host is always black . . . or blue . . . I'm still confused). At one point I was fiddling with my earring and Chris Kelly was basically hitting the card off camera to show me it was my line—it was only three seconds, but it felt like three hours. It was so bad I can't even look at it to this day, and all I kept thinking was *Yeah, they're never gonna give me another sketch again.*

But then something magical happened. There are moments at *SNL* I cherish because of the support I was shown—this was one of those moments. Every cast member, every director, even Lorne, everybody came over to tell me that's just the way it can sometimes go. "Welcome to live," everyone said. I was already being torn apart in the reviews—I kept breaking, which you really can't do. Even Higgins had said, "Barking dogs don't stop parades—you're fine."

But that night of the Chris Rock sketch I got the best love from Vanessa Bayer. She came over to sit next to me.

"Guess what?" she said.

"What?"

"You'll never do it again. That's the one advantage of what you just went through—after that, it'll never happen again."

And it didn't. Vanessa's words helped me get back out there and learn. As I've said, I learned a lot at *SNL*—I would never take that away from that place. You learn how to write there. You learn how to direct there. You learn how to cast there.

There was never a show that Kenan wouldn't go out to warm up the crowd by singing "Gimme some loving, every Saturday," and we'd be all singing along backstage at our stations. That meant the show was starting, and no show ever got boring to me. Even if I wasn't in it, or I was pissed, every show was still exciting. The table reads were something to look forward to. Being inside and warm and toasty in New York when it's snowing outside, on writing night someone shouts "the food is here," and it's a homey little family for a few hours while we work. Fridays, if we knew we had a couple of hours to waste, some of us would smoke or watch TV or go and fuck with people while they were doing their rehearsals. Or I'd go to a music rehearsal—I remember losing my shit on Bruno Mars, on Katy Perry. Prince? I got to see Prince. (I'll never forget Prince being on *SNL*; at one point he saw me to the side of the stage and because the room was dark, he thought I was Chris Rock. I know that because he called me Chris Rock.)

———————

SNL doesn't faze everyone. Take someone like Kenan Thompson. Kenan is a very calm person and a very loyal person. He's no pushover, don't get me wrong, but given his personality, I think it's easier for him to be settled into his place at *SNL*. And he's *also* very talented.

It's different for me. A Black woman is fighting for a life in that place. I had been through the *Ghostbusters* shit, been through the nudes and the Emmys, all that, and they could see that I was smarter than they knew. But still it took two or three seasons before they even started putting me in sketches.

After being there for a while, working at *SNL* could sometimes feel like high school. There were the popular people, and then the people who had to work to get popular. The writers tended to only use me for their shit, not for what I wanted to do—and to make it worse, they'd acted like they were really trying to get me material that was right for me, when in reality it never really happened. They ended up making me a caricature of myself, where *all* I did was beat people up, or chase someone, or be fucking someone. I ended up half-ass reading them, so they knew I wasn't up for it. In the end I had to start writing my own sketches just to get past these stereotypes—the big Black woman with the white woman, the big Black woman with the attitude, the big Black woman beating up somebody.

I can guess what you might say: *Weren't you grateful for the platform?* Of course I was, and all of those things were great when I started but I was more than they were trying to make me. And a lot of other shit happened—mental and physical stuff that I can't even tell you about because I know what will happen: As ever, I will be the drama.

There were a few people that made the job even crazier to the point where a bitch had to show her Compton side. One Tuesday writing night I got so mad at somebody's antics that I thought I was going to kill them, so I called an old friend from my Compton days. Let me tell you something: How much you come back when shit like this happens! My brain went all the way back to 1987, to Crips on the corner.

This muthafucka dies.

"Homeboy," I said, "I need you to fly in from Cali and put a bullet in a guy's head."

This dude is hardcore, let me tell you. There was a moment of silence.

"Babe," my contact said.

"What?!" I shouted.

"I just had a kid. And it's Christmas! You really want me to come? I'm wrapping presents—"

"Yes!" I shouted, a little less certainly.

And this was when I realized I was now really famous.

"Leslie," he said, "you know they gonna know you did it. Right? We all goin' to jail. Don't get me wrong, I'll do it. I mean, I'll come out. But damn, I just had a kid, and I gotta put the tree up and everything . . ."

We just busted out laughing.

"Yeah, I guess I can't kill him, huh?" I said.

"You think?" he said, laughing some more. "Maybe back in the day, but not anymore . . . Why don't you just

sucker-punch that muthafucka or something? You don't
need to kill him."

Then he said something really profound about me.

"You could kill him in another way though, Les, because
people just hate not even being in a real relationship with
you. It's a form of death. It is cold in your darkness."

Everybody thinks that if they're under this umbrella
with me, if I get mad eventually, I'm OK and I'll come
around. But there's only certain people I do that with. And
some people would make the mistake of thinking they were
one of them; some people take your kindness as weakness.

Despite everything that was going on, I still wanted to
be a team player, so I decided to write an ensemble sketch. It
was always fun for everyone to be in a sketch at the same
time, but they're hard to write so there are very few of them.
I knew, though, that if I wrote a great one, it would get on
because there were so few of them and they were hard to get
right. I figured that when they saw me create that for the
cast, they'd finally know I was, indeed, a team player. It
couldn't miss. But it wouldn't end well—it would lead to the
beginning of the end.

Fortunately, there were plenty of people at *SNL* who were
smart and respectful, especially the cast. I was closer to
some more than others, but for the most part we all got
along. Dina Morales was a producer who was always there
to support the cast if we needed anything. Jeff Blake and

Grace Shaker . . . angels! Don King, one of the directors, was hella cool, too. Gena Rositano and Chris Kelly, who ran the floor, were great to work with. Dale and Tom and Eric in wardrobe understood who and what I was. So many days they calmed me down. The costume dressers were the bomb, too. And then there is my glam team. This is my family. My stylist, Brian McPhatter, my hairstylist, Dennis Bailey; my makeup artist, Lola Okanlawon—they all been with me almost ten years. They are my ride or die crew for real. Lauren Roseman put out so many fires as a publicist. The thing they all had in common, though, was that they all saw me as Leslie; they didn't try to make me into someone else.

I think I upset a lot of people by being myself, actually. I just wasn't the one who didn't say something. I wasn't a spring chicken. So yes, if I thought something wasn't right, I spoke up about it. And some things I felt weren't right. For example, at one of my first pre-tapes in my first season at *SNL*, I fought for us to get dressing rooms. We often did those pre-tapes in really cold places, like by the river. I arrived that day and saw Kate sitting on the floor—an Emmy Award–winning actor, sitting on a fucking cold-ass concrete floor.

"Where are the dressing rooms?" I said.

"I don't know, bitch," Kate said using our nickname for each other. "This is how it is."

I acted as though I was leaving to get a cab because I was. The stage manager ran after me.

"Where you going?" she said.

"Ummm, home!" I said. "Where there's some heat and food. This how y'all treat the cast? I'm not gonna be in this video if that's the case." From that point, I was always on them about how they treated the cast, and sometimes that made me unpopular.

Fortunately, there was a different host every week who could break up the monotony of dealing with all this shit. The best tended to be the people who'd worked there or had hosted before. Kristen Wiig, for example—I watched Kristen just nail a really difficult sketch, to perfection, first time; that takes real talent. Steve Buscemi, Paul Rudd, Maya Rudolph, Alec Baldwin, all great.

Fred Armisen was one of the best, too. Honestly, I think Fred Armisen and I are supposed to be married. We click without even talking sometimes. On set we give them stuff they never dreamed they'd ever get. And Fred is a comedic beast.

Tom Hanks is a pro, of course, and he really taught me how to be a celebrity. When fans meet celebrities, they can tend to become temporarily insane. But Tom is just so normal. When I met him at *SNL* I immediately started into my feelings about *Philadelphia* and *Forrest Gump*, reciting lines at him, telling him what he did in the movie, like he didn't know. As I was fawning over him, he was giving me this kind of kindly side-eye.

"Leslie," he said, "you sound like a fangirl." I laughed and caught myself.

As we were sitting there, Jim Carrey happened to come by—it was the time he had that full beard. That was so sexy to me, so I figured I'd tell him so—not just that, I fully grabbed him by it.

"This is really working for me!" I said.

Tom and Jim just looked at me and laughed because I literally had no censor. Tom just looked at me and said, "That's the Leslie Jones I want to talk to." Lesson learned. Celebrities are just people; we know you love us; just be yourself.

Then there was Chance the Rapper. He is a prime example of being a Great Black Man. He loves his Black people, and he's so smart and incredibly talented. I was really happy that he knew who I was, too—that was so cool, and of course I invited him to smoke.

But he might not have known that he was being invited to smoke with grown folks. After the first joint I fired up another; Chance said, "This is pretty strong . . . Another one?"

Basically, I smoked him out. Let's just say we couldn't find Chance for a minute—he was fully knocked out in the wardrobe room.

Then there was someone like Miley Cyrus. So many people try to hate on her, but let me tell you, she is one of the gangsterist bitches I've ever met. For a start she is talented as fuck, and so grown.

"You're not a child at all," I said. I first met her when she hosted in October 2015, when she was just shy of her twenty-second birthday, and she had impressed me with how tough and mature she was.

"I don't think I had time to be a child," she said.

A few years later, during the *SNL* fortieth anniversary week, I watched her nail Paul Simon's "50 Ways to Leave Your Lover" in rehearsal. She hit one amazing note, caught my eye, and winked at me. That's Miley—gangster as fuck.

The Rock was the host of the first show in which I ever got to say "Live from New York . . ." I did a whole pre-tape with Reese Witherspoon that never made it to air about my inner white woman. Peter Dinklage was amazing.

Then there was Beyoncé . . . I got pictures with her, but I always fucked up the selfies—she'd look amazing, of course, but I'd always look like a maniac. One week she came by my station, made a heart sign, and said to me, "I love your work, sis . . ."

We all screamed; everyone was so jealous of me. But once again I fucked up the photos.

Then there are those people who go above and beyond.

I had a friend whose daughter was having a really hard time at school. Her father brought her to New York during Lady Gaga's week. The girl was a huge fan of Gaga, and I organized a meeting.

"I love you," the girl said when she met her.

Gaga said, "No, fuck that. You are a human. Look at yourself. This life ain't about what people say about you. What do you feel about yourself? That's what matters."

She broke it the fuck down for that girl.

"I will love you for the rest of my life," I said to Gaga afterwards. And that former little girl is now a really successful woman—she went on to be a *boss* . . .

Woody Harrelson was one of my favorites, too, because I think he's one of the best actors on earth. But his week of rehearsal he was smoking weed and his timing was a bit off. But the second the camera turned on, he *killed*! We were screaming at him backstage about how great he was.

"Did you guys think I was going to do badly?" he said, calmly.

But my absolute top favorite was Blake Shelton. Blake is a big-ass walking teddy bear. He hugs everybody and is hilarious . . . and he's older. That's a compliment—he's older, like me, so he *knows* shit. He's from Memphis, too, and knew everything from the classic *Hee Haw* TV show of my childhood—these New Yorkers didn't even know half the shit he knew. At one point I asked him if he remembered a song, and I started singing it at him:

"Where oh where are you tonight? Why did you leave me here all alone? I searched the world over . . ."

And sure enough, he just got his guitar and played that old song all the way through.

"You met another and *phfft* you were gone . . ."

I was crying.

"I thought I made that song up in my head!" I said.

"No, ma'am," he said.

Blake wanted to do a *Hee Haw* sketch as part of his opening monologue, too, but he was insisting that everybody would be in blond pigtails. I told him there was no way I was doing that.

He slid over to me. Let me tell you, Blake is a gorgeous-looking human.

"Please, Leslie," he whispered, "please wear the pigtails . . ."

I could not resist that man.

"Fuck!" I shouted, and I put them on . . . and it ended up being hilarious, partly because I was so mad he got me to wear them. I thought I looked ridiculous. You can see me out on the right of the sketch, glowering, but if you look closely, you can also see me trying not to laugh, too.

Blake wasn't the first person to enjoy how mad I can get. It's like an Aunt Esther thing from *Sanford and Son*— sometimes when I get really mad, people know I am mad, but I am also hilarious, so it's hard to keep from laughing when I am going off. People would have to get up and walk out because I would be livid, but I'd be saying some funny shit at the same time. This sketch in the pigtails was one of those times. They even played off me not wanting to be up there in pigtails.

"May I be excused?" I shout at one point as they tell old-ass jokes, "I do not like this!" and "This is wrong!" until finally they make fun of Blake, I laugh, and then Blake gets to shout, "We made Leslie laugh!"

There were great hosts, and some not so great hosts, too. It didn't really matter—I enjoyed all of them.

———————

What I've discovered is that mixing things up helps me get outside of myself, so for a long time I'd thought about using a writer to help me see things in a fresh way.

I had a couple of writers help me take my set more mainstream, find other branches to joke. People are so insecure in this business—me included, because I had to learn how to work with a writer. We don't help each other enough because people are fearful of losing their jobs. I think people need to write together; I have no problem with it now. Writers keep it honest with me about my material, keep it organized. We work on the jokes, expand on them. A good writer is my second ear. It's like having another you in the audience watching yourself.

I had a couple of writers I worked with before me and Lenny Marcus found each other.

I met Lenny at the Comedy Cellar—that night he was going up, and in between sets he was worrying over his girlfriend and whether or not he should marry her. Now, Lenny is a lot of things, but mostly he's a nerd—not a bad looking guy at all, just a nerd!—and Gina is incredibly beautiful, so we were all yelling at him to stop delaying. (By the way, anyone who knows a lot of words, or wears glasses, or is organized, or can answer a question I ask them on any random subject . . . that's a nerd.) But beyond his love life, it was just cool to sit and talk to someone my age, someone who gets it, someone I don't have to tell to be grown.

A year later I saw Lenny again and he'd done the right thing—he'd married Gina. We were watching a Yankees game on TV that night, and I offered to take him to Yankee Stadium (I had access to Lorne's seats behind home plate). That night at the game we laughed so hard. Lenny had already given me some notes on a couple of my jokes, and I really liked what he had to say. He was really organized about it, had written it all up like a book report—this bit can go here, this bit can go there—and that night at the game it was so great just to have an adult to talk to, someone paying their own bills and not asking me for money or a job. That night I realized he should open for me. I've always tried to be that comic who helps out other comics.

Lenny first opened for me at the Talking Stick Casino in Arizona in January 2018. That first night, I figured, *Lenny's gonna love me, man. Lenny's gonna be like, this bitch can do so much time.*

So I did one hour and twenty minutes.

That's a long time.

I came off the stage doing that cocky, I-just-did-an-hour-and-twenty-minutes walk.

Lenny said, "What was that? Who needs to watch a comedian for an hour and twenty minutes? Get your ass off the stage—fifty-eight minutes, tops. When they give the credit cards back, you should be closing your set."

No one had ever talked to me like that.

"But, how are you not impressed? You're not impressed by me? You don't know how it goes . . ."

"I know how it goes," Lenny said. "If I paid for that ticket and your ass did an hour twenty minutes? I would never pay to see you again!"

It didn't stop there. Back at the hotel Lenny kept going.

"You said muthafucka fifty-two times," he said. "I counted." He'd noted down on a piece of paper every curse word I said and how many times I said it.

"You're scaring me now," I said. "You're Rain Man. Muthafucka, it's absolutely terrifying."

"I'm not scaring you," he said. "I'm telling you that if you have this many curse words, how many regular words do you have? I can't even understand the joke because there's so many *muthafucka*s in it. The curse words muddle the real words."

What I realized was that Lenny is a serious student of the job. He had taken it on himself to break my shit down.

"You are very talented," he said, "maybe a unicorn. You may be a savant, but you are all over the place. I can't remember any of your shit . . ."

It was clear he was deadly serious.

"Where's your set list?" he said.

"Nah," I said, "I stopped doing set lists a long time ago."

"Dude," he said, "the Rolling Stones have a set list."

From that point on, when I went out onstage he would give me a piece of paper, and every time I would fold it up and put it on the bench and just do what I wanted to. After the show I would come offstage and say, "Well, that joke didn't work."

"You know why it didn't work, right? Because the real joke is on the paper." Often Lenny would yell at me for a half an hour after each show—it got so bad that I had to commit to doing everything on the goddamn set list . . . and discovered that in doing so I destroyed in a way that was very comfortable and easy and—dare I say it—very organized. I didn't struggle to try to remember shit. Sometimes I'd have fun with it, telling the audience, "My writer wants me to look at this paper—he has a whole show on here." Everybody would laugh, and Lenny would be in the back with his head in his hands.

I've taken that nerd everywhere with me ever since.

As I've said, I really wanted to show that I was a team player at *SNL*, and one of the best ways to do that was to create a sketch everyone could be in. I came up with the idea and me and Lenny had stayed up all night Tuesday writing it. The joke was, everyone in the cast was going to get drunk and get tattoos, then we'd all wake up sober the next day and see what tattoos we'd gotten.

Kate, being gay, had been given a huge penis on her back (she thought this was hilarious). Che has a big tattoo of Colin on his back, and vice versa. Mine was just "Annette," which, though it is my real name, I hate.

Simple gag, but a good one, and it used the whole cast. But after I'd turned it in, Erik Kenward told me it was mean, and they weren't going to run with it.

So I hit Lorne on text.

"I don't understand," I wrote. "I'm really trying. I wrote a sketch for the whole crew and I don't understand . . .

Lorne wrote back that he was concerned that I'd used Lenny, an outside writer they couldn't vouch for.

"I wrote that sketch!" I said. "Lenny just helped me *form* it, and people use writers from outside all the time. You let muthafuckas get away with this shit all the time," I said.

This was the biggest fight Lorne and I ever had. At the next table read I just flung the scripts across the room and walked out. I talked shit all the way to the elevator—"Y'all can take these sketches and shove 'em up your fuckin' ass..."

NBC expected me to be on that show every week, but I was done. I refused to come in. Who were they going to send to my house to get me?

Lorne texted me: "Are you coming in?"

Nope. Me being so angry took all the joy out of the building. It was like that for two weeks.

Lorne and I were always real with each other; and I knew he understood, but *SNL* is its own world—of which he's the puppet master—and they weren't going to just change it for me. I'm sure it was frustrating for him to see me frustrated. Now, looking back on it, I can see it with rested eyes. I'm sure Lorne had reasons for not being able to support me every time. The bottom line is, he gave me an extraordinary opportunity, which led to so many incredible things.

The Idris Elba show was my last. I remember telling Idris I was done, and he didn't believe me; Meek Mill didn't believe me, either, when I'd told him during what we call "Good-nights," the end of the show where everyone is onstage with the host. That whole final week, even during table read, I found myself crying . . . but as ever, *SNL* doesn't take shit like that seriously. Their attitude is "Everybody always says they're going to leave but then they're back the next season."

Well, I say what I mean. And I mean what I say.

So, reading for my last sketch with Kyle Mooney, we were singing the Carpenters song "Close to You," and once again I found myself crying as I was singing. The only person who came up to me afterwards was Kenan. It hurt that no one else said anything.

"It's so disrespectful," I told him.

"This is how they are," he said. "They don't believe that you're leaving."

But I was, and I did. Season 44, 2018–19, was my last.

Saturday Night Live is its own universe, and no matter how much you try to change the status quo, some things are going to stay the same. Knowing that, I had to remember that one of those things I would always do, no matter how difficult the situation I found myself in, was to work harder than anyone else. People think when you leave it is a failure, but I don't consider my time at *SNL* as a failure. I consider it part of my journey of becoming who I am. I was successful there, and I accomplished a lot. It was just my time to move on. It will always hold a special place in my heart. I know *SNL* will always be *SNL*.

I texted and emailed Lorne two months before I left to thank him for the opportunity but that I was leaving at the end of season 44.

I knew I wouldn't get an answer. And that was that.

New York was killing me, too—not to mention I had more injuries at *SNL* than I did playing basketball for fifteen years. I was done with all of it.

I would discover, though, that I would reach a whole different level after *SNL*.

Chapter Thirteen

ROID RAGE

I am sick of being nice.

It does not work for me to sugarcoat things.

I kept thinking back to what Lorne said when he hired me: "I don't know what you are, but I know that I want you here. You're something I never knew I needed." And yet what happened at *SNL* has happened so many times to me: People hire me because I'm Leslie Jones, but then they don't actually know what that is, so they try to turn me into something else.

That's what is so frustrating about this business. They want you to be different but still fit into the status quo. When I started, I was all about following the Hollywood plan. I did my hair, I lost the weight, I took the classes, I got the manager and the agents, and really worked on my craft. I did all "the things," and still didn't make it. I followed all the rules and if I was gonna make it their way, I would have done so in my twenties and thirties—I was just as funny then as I am now. But I didn't make it. So, I had to do the work of finding out what I was and where I fit in this industry.

I remember hearing Diana Ross once say, "Know who you are because if you don't, they will make you what they want." And that was the mistake I was making—I was waiting for Hollywood to make me, but it was never supposed to be that way. I have a bigger purpose.

What I try to explain to people is, you are gonna fail. But failing helps you recognize success. Failure is not bad, but I'm also not glamorizing it. I'm glamorizing growing. I think if I had made it earlier, I would not be who I am today, because I would have stopped growing, and may not have reached the full potential I was capable of. We sometimes rush to make it instead of respecting the journey. Jamie Foxx was so right about living life, having all the experiences, all the hurts, the rejection, the happiness, the sadness.

It all goes together to make up who you are. Go through it all—it's yours. You should love it and own it as yours. It's what helps you love yourself, and all of you, not just the good parts. You may not be perfect, but you are somebody, and you have a story. You don't need to be anyone but who you are. So many of us are trying to escape from who we are. Stand in yourself. I swear, if you start that work, you will be amazed to find out you are awesome. There is only one you.

I didn't discover that I was special at SNL—I was always that. I just had not fully owned it. And that's the frustration with this industry—you have to fight for that freedom, and when you do, sometimes it's a problem, especially if they want to take your magic and use it the way *they* want you to use it. Or they just try to own your magic, or wring the fuck out of it, or try to copy it. Or they will try to make you think they discovered your magic.

The point is, no matter where I go, I will be Leslie Jones. I'm talented in spite of the bullshit. I will be successful at anything you give me to do because of my talent. No one can own that or take it away. And you got to be willing to walk away from something that is not for you, no matter how big it is. I don't stay anywhere I'm not wanted. I don't let people misuse me anymore—I don't have to. My talent can take me anywhere I want to go. I'm not conceited or cocky. I'm just convinced.

Trust me, you have to fight to get to that point. I would continue to get tested. It happens all the time. Take the live tweeting of the Olympics as a perfect example.

I'm just sitting and watching TV and tweeting my love for those incredible athletes for y'all, and for free. No one helps me with that. I do everything myself. But then NBC started to give me a hard time about rights to the clips I was referencing. Again, it's people thinking my talent is a fluke, or it's impossible for me to be that funny, or they think that they can copy what I do, but what they don't understand is that what they're seeing is real passion. I am incredibly passionate about the skills of Olympians—those athletes are incredible, and it brings me so much joy to watch them and that's what comes across when I tweet. You can't fake that, or own it! It means so much to me still because it's something that me and my dad used to share—we'd watch every single minute of every

Olympics together. (How many of y'all watched the Olympics with your loved ones?) But OK, you think you can get other people to do the same thing I do? No, you can't, because when I do it, I come from an innocent, passionate place that goes all the way back to my childhood.

I've done a bunch of stuff since *SNL*—including the movie *Coming 2 America* and my Netflix special, *Time Machine*— but sometimes I found that I would be hired to be me, but then I wasn't allowed to be me.

During one conversation with my agents I just happened to tell the story of when, years earlier, my friend and I auditioned for *Supermarket Sweep*.

I took that shit seriously back then—I recorded the shows, and I trained my friend how to play. On the day of audition, I told her to take the day off, but she still scheduled to go into work later that day—what's worse was that she was just supposed to be covering someone else's shift! She was under the impression that TV people, like other industries, went home at five p.m. . . .

As the audition progressed, it was clear that we're good as shit. We were *killing*, and we made it to the final round. But if we missed the final round, we would be done; they'd never pick us.

"I have to leave!" my friend said.

"We're killing!" I said. "You have to stay. We have a chance to win."

It was late now—they would have to put us last because we were obviously the best.

But there was nothing I could do—she had to go to work. I walked out to the bus stop, and she walked to her car. I called her every name in the book on the way. I didn't even want to ride with her I was so mad.

So when I told my agents this story, they lit up.

"We'll go after it!" they said. "*Supermarket Sweep* is Leslie Jones's life dream!"

But the truth was, I watched it back when I didn't have a job, just like I watched *The Price Is Right* and *Wheel of Fortune*. It wasn't the dream of my life. But then I thought, *Well, I could give money away to people*, which *was* a life dream, so I agreed to do it.

———————

To celebrate I took myself to London for a vacation at the end of 2019, at Christmastime.

And that was the last good moment for me for a while. Because something was going on with my health.

For years I'd suffered from really bad hemorrhoids. Let me tell you, of all the funny things in this book, hemorrhoids are no joke. My doctor had been trying to avoid surgery for as long as possible—she'd been doing this thing called banding, where she would tie a rubber band around the base of these things and choke off their blood supply . . . until they died, and just fell out your ass. Yes, that's just as excruciatingly painful as it sounds.

The first time I went in to see her she mentioned that there may be a couple more that she thought, but the second time? She emerged from my ass all sweaty, like she had been in a war.

"They're everywhere," she panted. "Everywhere. I tried to shoot 'em and they just kept coming . . ."

All this was happening in my ass.

I went off to London, but when I got back, the doctor said I had to have surgery. It was planned for February 12, 2020. By then, there was this new virus thing starting to generate headlines across the world—Britain had just seen its first case, and there were fourteen confirmed in the US.

As I say, I'd suffered for years from hemorrhoids. I'd never had any money to get it fixed, and living in New York hadn't helped, given that I'd been so stressed and eating poorly. When they finally did the surgery in February, the doctor said it was way worse than she'd realized—she'd had to cut them in quarters just to get them out. That's fucked up.

Post-surgery, I went through hell. It took me two months to get better, right as the world shut down for COVID-19. My Aunt Pat came out to stay with me for a week, but let me tell you, learning how to shit again?

The only way I got through all of that pain was to use my imagination and create a mental animation for what was happening inside my butt.

Let me explain.

Remember that movie *Osmosis Jones*, where Chris Rock plays a white blood cell wandering about inside a human body? That's where I got the inspiration for Merle.

Merle is an imaginary dude who lives and works in my ass.

He may be imaginary, but I know what he looks like and everything. Merle has those big glasses and crazy hair and a little suit. Merle is a soldier for the job. He's been with me ever since these hemorrhoids arrived, and he's handled that area valiantly and carefully. But Merle has no life. Oh, sure, he has a wife and kids and a house, but he has to live/work in my ass, in that shitty little office (literally), and he never gets to see his family. His wife almost divorced him.

Somebody else had to teach his kids how to ride a bike.

But now, with the hemorrhoids gone, Merle was like, "OK, so it's a whole new program down here. Your ass is numb, so I'm a gonna take a much-needed vacation with my wife."

They went to the DR; he came back all suntanned and everything.

As for me, well, sure enough, it was a whole new system down there—and I wasn't shitting correctly. But once he got back from the DR, all relaxed and fully rested, Merle was there all along, checking everything, connecting sensors. Your body is way smarter than you are—it understands that once the hemorrhoids are gone, all the ass sensors need to be checked, because they are going crazy. It was Merle's job to get all those sensors working together.

The point is, this was the most horrific part of my life. When I say "spasms in the ass," let me just say that it's something you will never in your life ever want to feel. It feels like somebody took Thor's muthafuckin' hammer and is just literally hitting the top of your coccyx. I couldn't sleep because whenever I would relax, that's when the spasms hit. I was clenched up constantly. The only time I got any relief was when I was in water, so I would take ten baths a day.

All this was happening while the world slowly but surely shut the fuck down. I didn't have a clue. All I knew was my bedroom, my bathtub, and the toilet seat. I wasn't eating anything except oranges and chicken.

Eventually the sensors would tell me it was time to go, and oh my god. Did I mention that I had a bunch of sutures in my ass? I had a bunch of sutures. In. My. Ass. When I went, it felt like shitting razor blades. Even the tiniest poo felt like I was giving birth to a fifteen-pound baby. With the hemorrhoids out, the canal is small again, so my body was having to learn how to stretch once more. So every piece of shit that comes out of me, I am birthing it; I was having shit babies.

And then Merle said, "Boss lady, I haven't wanted to tell you this. But there's a bunch of shit that has got to come out. And there will be seven of them. You're going to have seven shit babies."

Seven is a very biblical number, but what happened next made me question the existence of God.

The first shit was murder, pure and simple. Second, manslaughter, but still. Third, assault with a deadly weapon. Fourth, fifth, and sixth were a tiny bit better, but still crazy painful.

And then the seventh, sweet hallelujah, the seventh was . . . normal.

It was three o'clock in the morning. I was so depressed. I'm having shit babies. I'm old. I'm tired. This is my body.

All night I'd been getting texts from people about something that was happening online, but I was in no state to pay attention.

And even though I wasn't in pain anymore, I was still crying, still unable to sleep. I figured I should at least check out what all these texts I'd been getting were about.

I opened up my computer, and there was DJ D-Nice hosting his epic, legendary dance party in the middle of the world being locked down. It was Friday, March 20.

I felt a huge smile working its way across my face. I was crying, but I wasn't about to let the world defeat me. I needed to stay undeniable.

So I started to dance, along with millions of people around the world, and I danced until eight o'clock in the morning.

"Last night a DJ saved my life . . ."

—————————

We made *Supermarket Sweep* during COVID. I could kinda see the problems going in, but I truly was positive about doing it. After *SNL*, I knew I had to go into a situation and learn the system first. I had never hosted a game show, so I was eager to learn. But on my journey in this business, I also learned what "world-renowned" means. When you hear that phrase, run, because it means nothing! Every time I work with a so-called "world-renowned," it is a complete disaster. It happens in hair, makeup, glam, directors, productions—every time. Most people in this industry live in a bubble, so titles get you through more than talent. But most times, when I get a "world-renowned," I ask them, "Hey, have you been to Compton? That's the part of the world I'm from." I respect a person who can kill at their craft. That is what is expected of me—to show up and be Leslie Jones—so I expect everyone else to be at that same level. If you say you know what you are doing and I trust you, but then you turn out to not be as good as you are "renowned" to be, then I'm gonna tell you. I don't half-ass anything.

At *Supermarket Sweep* we were told we would be working with the best, but honestly, how would we know? I'd never been in the game show world before. It was after COVID had started, so we rehearsed on Zoom for twenty-seven weeks, and for the most part it was going great. I didn't agree with some of the decisions, but I was told to just trust them, so I did. We were taping a really funny show.

Once we did the tapings they sent us the edits, but they had cut all the funny stuff out. Lenny saw it first, and one night he texted me really late—and Lenny never texts me in the middle of the night.

"I need you to look at this," he said. "And call me afterwards, please."

So I looked at the edit, and I was just horrified. We had rehearsed for twenty-seven weeks, and they sent us dogshit. It was as if they were trying to prove to me that they could do the show without me or my comedy. They took out all the joy, all the sketches, all the jokes. Why the fuck did you hire me then, if you didn't want me?! I was not only furious, I was insulted. Once again, I'm being told, "We are going to change you into what *we* want."

It was so awful. At the next Zoom meeting, they told me they'd fix it, but I wanted Lenny to edit the show. I felt like it was time to take my business back, to let me show them what Leslie is. Stop trying to stuff me in a box. If you're hiring me for me, then you are gonna get me! If we had released the show those first *producers* had edited, it would have failed. And it's my name that's at stake. They agreed to let us do it—I wasn't giving them much choice because we were executive producers—so Lenny and I did the edit with the *editors* of the show.

It was one of the hardest thing I've ever done. We became best friends with the editors and we created some great material.

After season one of *Supermarket Sweep*, I was hired to do an Uber Eats commercial. Sigh . . .

You know everyone wants to be famous, and yes, it's nice at times, but it is never what you expect. Yes, the money is great, but sometimes these jobs can make you feel like a racehorse. You have to trust folks to look out for you, and be on same page. It can be exhausting. It seriously comes down to a trust thing, and sometimes those very people you need to look out for you let you down. My manager had no idea what was happening with the ad, no schedule, nothing. At the end of a very long first-day shoot, I was told I had to sit for a bunch of still photos. Again, my manager had no idea I'd been put up for this, and it wasn't like it was just regular stills—they wanted faces and attitude and positioned poses, all that. This is after nine or ten hours.

Honestly, my manager should have shut that shit down, but I'm a pro, so I started mugging for the camera, giving them what they wanted. At one point, I had my face in a certain way, and the guy behind the photographer said, "Yeah, do that again. Bug your eyes again . . ."

For the people who don't know, "bug your eyes" is a derogatory term that goes all the way back to blackface. It's fucking offensive.

I said, "What did you say?"

He repeated himself.

"Bug your eyes. Bug your eyes again."

At this point, my makeup artist ran from the monitor, shouting, "Shut this down! You don't say that to her."

I'd said nothing because I was in complete shock. I couldn't believe he said it . . . and then repeated it. My manager? Just standing there, not saying anything.

People say to me all the time, "You are loyal to a fault," and I am. Nothing wrong with being loyal, but when it starts to harm you, you got to know when to let go because you are not helping either one if you don't. I learned this lesson so many times in my life, with my father, Richard, my brother, writers, some close friends—all heartbreaking—and now, my longtime manager.

After getting through the first season of *Sweep*, we had committed to a second season. It was supposed to be easy, but we ended up doing four shows a day, which honestly almost killed me. They no longer wanted to feed the crew, either, because they were making budget cuts, but those folks had been there from six in the morning, and all they'd been offered was a rubbery bagel. By the time I was done yelling, they'd gotten them one of the best food services—all kinds of food trucks had been hired.

We had worked very hard with those editors and had created a system where it worked. But eventually some new people came in and said that we'd been doing it all wrong and that *they* could do it better, completely disrespecting the editors' work, and me. It was a mess! "World-renowned" my ass! And if you know me, I had a lot to say. My name is on this—I mean, I was an executive producer, for crying out loud—so yeah, I went the fuck off. But I definitely played right into what they wanted by cursing them out, and after the second season of *Sweep*, we reached an impasse and decided not to make any more seasons.

In the end, it turns out they wanted a host, but not Leslie Jones.

People seem to expect some kind of distant, unconnected, unrelatable robot to show up, but I care about the people who work around me. When I fight for people to get paid, or fed, I run the risk of looking difficult, especially as I'm a tall-ass Black woman with a trumpet voice. But I'm the magic, and if my name is on it I'm going to fight for what's right. And honestly, to know me is to love me!

When you're a comedian, that skill that you develop means that eventually you'll learn to be funny no matter where you are.

When the pandemic showed up, I was one of the fortunate ones. I didn't have to worry about paying my bills or risking my life to go to work; I was just sitting in my house like everyone else. When I hadn't been preparing for *Sweep* on Zoom I was watching all this terrible stuff happen. But I'm a comedian, so I know how to pull diamonds out of shit.

Each day, like so many of us, I found myself watching the news, and specifically, I started to get obsessed with the reporters doing their jobs out of their own homes. It didn't take me long to realize that a lot of these people hadn't really thought through their home environments. Does this bitch know she has a can of Coke up on a shelf? Look at that— that's half a sandwich right there. And the backgrounds that people chose for their appearances! Steve Schmidt, for example—every one of his backdrops was as freaky as fuck. There were pools, crystal palaces, all sorts of weird shit—the backgrounds were one of the best things about watching him.

Riffing on all this felt just like crowd work. What I really loved was when people knew I was talking about them, and they'd do something specially for me in the background. I'd complimented one guy about his flowers—sure enough, every day, more flowers. Then a guy started wearing ties because I'd liked his tie one day.

Then there was Adam Schiff—I swear he's from the past. That is a dude who is truly quantum leaping. He's got Ben Franklin's rocking chair in the corner, for fuck's sake . . .

In the process of watching so much political TV, I was starting to really learn about the subject. I had already started learning a little bit about politics at *SNL*, and what I realized was that we just haven't been doing our job as citizens. Not nearly enough of us vote and it feels like everybody is so complacent. And when you don't pay attention, that's when you get scammed—we're getting scammed by politicians! (What are they doing with all the money for a start? Look at all these potholes! You almost fucked up my BMW.)

We have created so many systems for people not to make it in life—especially Black people. It's as if some Republicans don't want people to be successful. They need certain people to be poor, to be disenfranchised. They're banning books? You're not banning porn! And you'll trust teachers with guns but not with books? You say you want to protect kids, while making them have children they don't want or can't look after?

The problem is, in the past thirty or so years we've just stopped paying attention. As a people we've become lazy, so involved in our lives that we don't care about anything else; we're just functioning, waiting to die. All those old white muthafuckas have noticed our complacency, believe: "They don't care," they seem to say, "so we'll take away voting anyway—they won't even notice." But you're supposed to be involved in politics! Only a third of our country is voting. Even if it was a half, or two-thirds? We wouldn't be in trouble. Everyone knows we need to change gun laws and safeguard rights for women, protect and educate our kids, but what happens when twenty people order food for one hundred—you get what the twenty people wanted! So many of us think, *Well, one person can't do anything* . . . But do you know how many millions of people are saying that? We've forgotten that we live here, on this planet, together; the earth is a big-ass apartment complex, and we're not taking care of the complex.

We've become so scared and *tired* . . . Every report I saw—from MSNBC to Steve Kornacki's khakis—gave me a new insight. I've always felt that I wanted to be one of the performers who could help to interpret the world for people, and that's what it felt like here. Jon Stewart had done it, and Colin Quinn, too, and then it felt like it was my turn.

Getting so involved in politics really prepared me for my *Daily Show* stint in early 2023 after Trevor Noah quit. I went in there with a clear opinion and a mission.

When I say mission, I mean this: Sometimes I feel like the two-thousand-year-old woman. I've lived in the '60s, '70s, '80s, '90s, and now twenty years into the 2000s. I've been where you've been, and we've been through the same struggle, so I want to use what I've learned to make people more engaged in the political process. I feel like I have the right to say, "Listen to me. I'm here to talk about this shit. You're a man who needs to go to therapy? Let's talk about it! Planned Parenthood? Bring that shit out and let's talk about it!"

Plus, the writers on the *Daily Show* are so good, and it was so great to get to be funny about politics while also making a point. I got a great reaction to the bit I did about the restricted documents that keep showing up at politicians' houses. My point was, who in the fuck is giving these people the documents in the first place?

In the end, what I learned in the pandemic, and since, is what so many of us learned: life is life. It's not supposed to be easy all the time, and it's never as easy as we want it to be. But live through your trauma, stop running from yourself— you are your best friend. Think about it—would you let someone hurt your best friend? No. Do the same for yourself. You will get the biggest reward: happiness, even in a storm. Grant yourself some grace because life can be short, but it can be long as fuck, too. You wake up every day and you hope you make it back to your bed safely. You hope you get good sleep, and you hope you wake the fuck up. That's it.

WELCOME TO MY FUNERAL

I didn't attend the funerals of either of my parents, but that doesn't mean I don't think about my own.

I hope my death is really exciting. I don't want no bull-shit death. I don't want the conversation to go like this:

"How did Leslie Jones die?"

"Aw, she fell off her balcony."

"Did somebody push her?"

"No—her goofy ass was smoking weed and she got caught in the curtain and went over the edge."

Y'all better say somebody broke in and I fought furiously for my life, superhero like . . . but they took me out with a hammer.

Now that I'm famous, I have to think about this shit. You gotta think how these muthafuckas are gonna celebrate your death.

I do not want to be sitting through my own seven-hour funeral, muthafuckas. That's not what I want. I'm just trying to get to heaven ASAP to fuck Tupac.

So, I'm gonna tell you what I want for my funeral.

———————

It starts off with Jason Mimosas—you know the dude I'm talking about, the Drogo dude. He's going to have that whole Drogo hookup: no shirt, hair just flowing up on some distant mountaintop, and Russell Crowe will be standing next to him with a bow and arrow—and it's not the fat-ass Russell Crowe, either—I'm talking about the gladiator-suited Russell Crowe, him saying, "Are you ready to be entertained?"

Then, a camera will swoop down (I will fund the jib cameras, trust), to where a raft awaits on a lake, a raft made out of Chippendale strippers' uniforms and G-strings. COVID hit them real bad, so they have a lot of shit to get rid of.

On the raft, there I am, just lying there in my Christian Siriano purple dress, dead as a muthafucka.

Tongue out. (Tongue *not* out? Not dead.)

Now, in my original plans for my funeral, at this point I had Kanye and his choir starting to sing, but since he is tripping like a muthafucka, he is hereby disinvited. He will be replaced by Lizzo. I want her whole ass out, and I want her playing that muthafuckin' flute. Oh, and backed up by the Rihanna Super Bowl halftime dancers. Lizzo uses her whole butt to push the raft out into the water. Jason and Russell bring a flaming arrow, and Jason sends it in a great arc right out at me, and now I'm burning.

At this point, enter the Peruvian boy. I had previously imported him from Peruvia, and he has been training for this moment for his entire life. He learned how to swim from birth because he knew that one day, he would have to do this. (He will later go to the Olympics, thanks to me; it wasn't for nothing.) And he is standing by the shore with a gold cup in his hand, his whole family is surrounding him, murmuring, "Oh my God, Pedro . . ." And with that, Pedro from Peruvia enters the waters and swims with one hand in the air because he's holding the golden chalice. When he reaches my burned-out carcass, he scoops up all the ashes into the cup, then swims all the way back.

Lizzo continues to flute, Pedro gives the cup to Snoop Dogg, who then Crip-walks all the way to his lowrider and then drives to San Bernardino, where he gives it to my boy, Les, who has a weed factory. Les takes my ashes, puts them on the plant, and now I'm weed.

(Wait, I think I just snitched out my homeboy. Let's just call him "Lance.")

You're welcome. I'll be with you for the rest of my life. But you probably won't appreciate it, so fuck it, I'll smoke myself.

The lifeblood of my career is still doing my sets in clubs and working on bits like the one about my funeral. Nothing beats it—working the crowd, giving people shit, doing my stuff. Recently I asked some dude in the audience if he was married, and he said, "Yes, but I'm looking," and I killed that muthafucka for like ten minutes. I'm pretty sure he regretted being such an asshole, but probably not as much as his wife regrets marrying him. That's what I love: making people laugh at themselves. That couple will talk about that and laugh at themselves for a while. I love giving laughter to people.

But you have to respect comedy. You have to respect the craft; you are not better than the craft—it will go on after you are dead; you have to pay your dues; you have to learn from those who've gone before and who have experience. But most of all, work to be you. Find out where you really fit. Open yourself up to all new things—you never know where they lead. Yes, you might be afraid, but do it anyway. That's what courage is: still going for it, even when you are scared. And if I encourage even one person with my story, I'm happy.

Recently, I did a show at the Hollywood Bowl, and as I drove home that night, I couldn't help but think about what Willie Jones Jr had said to me all those years earlier: "Don't let anyone tell you that you're Black and you're a female and you can't do it. You can do whatever the fuck you want as long as you work hard . . . As long as you are better than everybody else, you'll get what you deserve . . . You are Black; you are female . . . That means that you are going to have to work harder than everybody else. But if you work harder you are undeniable. They can't deny you. They going to tell you that you are a woman, they're going to tell you that you're Black. They will say you can't make it. Don't fucking listen."

That night at the Bowl, I had heard the unmistakable sounds of people laughing at me, calling me "stupid" in a good way, lapping up what I was giving them. I had been undeniable.

This comedy world, like any other craft, tends to be a man-driven thing. I've suffered all the misogyny, all the doubts, but in spite of all that shit, you still gotta be "*that* muthafucka." Nobody can stop me but me.

Eventually I got home to my house in the Hills. After I parked, I waited for a minute, letting everything sink in. I was arriving at a four-thousand-square-foot house; it has a pool and a glam room and its very own version of a 7-Eleven, filled with candy and snacks and anything the fuck I want. This girl from Compton, arriving home from having just played in front of thousands in the Hollywood Bowl.

Undeniable.

I locked up the car and went into the house through the garage. Man, only the little girl in me with pigtails would appreciate this, and she was saying to me, *I can't believe this is our place. You got any money? Anything to eat? I know you gonna give me some of them shoes . . .*

And at that moment, when she smiled at me, it was clear—this kid would have to work harder than everybody else, and be better than everyone else, but when she did, she would become undeniable.

She would be me.

I wish my parents were alive to get the fruits of my labor, my brother, too. But when we meet again, I'm sure they'll have a bunch of stories to tell me. My brother will say, "What's crackin', cupcake?" My dad will say, "You are definitely undeniable."

My mom will say, "Why you didn't get married and have some grandkids?"

Acknowledgments

Like I said at the start, y'all know who y'all is . . .

About the Author

LESLIE JONES is a three-time Primetime Emmy Award nominee, as well as a Writers Guild of America Award and NAACP Image Award nominee for her work on *Saturday Night Live*. She has also been honored as one of *Time* magazine's 100 Most Influential People. Jones recently wrapped production on season 2 of the HBO Max series *Our Flag Means Death*. The week of January 17, 2023, Jones kicked off a new era of *The Daily Show* as the program's first guest host. In 2021, she starred opposite Eddie Murphy in *Coming 2 America*, for which she won an MTV Movie & TV Award and was nominated for a People's Choice Award. Jones will next produce an untitled Christmas comedy for Lionsgate, which she is currently developing as a potential future starring role. Additionally, Jones cohosts the podcast *The Fckry* with comedian Lenny Marcus. Each week, Jones and Marcus interview guests and answer listener questions, while exposing "the fckry" of any given topic.